Endorsements

The value of the prophetic gift to the Church cannot be overstated. Encouragement, timing, divine strategies, alerts regarding satan's schemes—these benefits and more flow from Holy Spirit to us through the prophetic gift. Gina Gholston's amazing dreams, visions, and prophecies deliver these benefits and more. Her broad knowledge of Scripture allows them to be delivered with revelatory teaching, strengthening their impact while simplifying their application…truly a unique mix. *Carry On* is a very helpful book for our times!

Dutch Sheets, Apostle
Best-selling Author

****

In my book, *Angel Armies on Assignment,* I described a vision and a word the Lord gave me regarding a division of angels. In the vision, the word He highlighted to me was "revival," but it was spelled re-vive-all. When I read Gina's manuscript, I knew that God was reemphasizing this prophetic word regarding revival and that angels were being activated to "revive all" in this season as we carry out and carry on His mandated assignments on each of our lives. He is writing us into His story, and Gina's book will challenge you to keep running the race as He activates the mantles on our lives and brings angel armies to assist.

Dr. Tim Sheets, Apostle
Author of *Angel Armies, Angel Armies on Assignment, New Era of Glory*

****

i

May we never forget what God has done and miss what God will do. Thank you, Gina, for the many priceless and powerful reminders in this book.

Ray Hughes
Author, Songwriter, Storyteller, Poet, Teacher

****

Gina Gholston's book, *Carry On*, is long overdue. Gina lays out a clarion call for all believers to wake up and possess their God-given inheritance! This is not just a book full of good information, but revelatory insight that will activate a generation into their destiny to serve, shake, and shock the world into the Kingdom of God!

Paul Owens, Pastor
Fresh Start Church
Peoria, Arizona

****

Gina's passion for revival and clarity of scripture is the solid foundation that sets the stage for a book that is making a mark in our quest for every church to be revived. Pastors in churches, small and large, are needing confirmation that God is speaking. She reveals that revival is in the foundation of our churches. Our job is to tap into that substratum and LET GOD MOVE. A must read.

Clint Knowles
Regional Bishop
Church of God of Prophecy
Ohio ~ West Virginia

****

When I first met Gina, I felt like I had known her my entire life. It was as if she sat on the second row of my childhood church. It is her transparency and relatability you will feel as you read her book. Her writings are much needed concerning the current state of the Body of Christ. This is a fresh revelation being birthed out of the historical foundations of Pentecost in America. This book is not only historical fact, but prophetic guidance for our next! Church…let us *Carry On*.

Elizabeth Knowles
Women's Ministries
Church of God of Prophecy
Ohio ~ West Virginia
Author of Your Morning Matters

****

Gina Gholston's book, *Carry On*, is a call to embrace the reality of our spiritual birthright, and it is a potent reminder that we are not just recipients of this divine legacy, but also its guardians. This sacred trust is ours to hold, ours to share, and ours to perpetuate across generations. It's a call to embody the divine flame that God has kindled within us, ensuring that its warmth and light reach not only those in our immediate sphere, but also those who will follow in our footsteps. This book is an empowering, spiritual manifesto that ignites within the reader a blazing awareness of their divine potential.

Alan DiDio
Host of Encounter Today

CARRY ON

Becoming Faithful Stewards of

Our Spiritual Inheritance

Gina Gholston

Carry On

Becoming Faithful Stewards of
Our Spiritual Inheritance

by Gina Gholston

Copyright © 2023 by Gina Gholston

Geneva Bible 1599 (GB) - Geneva Bible, 1599 Edition. Published by Tolle Lege Press. All rights reserved.

New American Standard Bible (NASB) - Copyright © 1960, 1962, 1963, 1968, 1971, 1972, 1973, 1975, 1977, 1995 by The Lockman Foundation. Used by permission.

Edit/Layout by Jim Bryson (JamesLBryson@Gmail.com)

Cover design by David Munoz (davidmunoznvtn@gmail.com)

Contents

Foreword 1

Introduction 3

1. Our Spiritual Inheritance 7

2. We've Got Oil 21

3. The Mantle of Revival 31

4. The Continuation 49

5. Movement in the Hill Country 65

6. Take Your Seat 75

7. A Big Picture Moment 91

8. Anchored in Hope 111

9. In His Grip 129

10. A Redemptive Movement 141

About the Author 153

More by Gina Gholston 155

Contact Info 157

Dedication

I DEDICATE THIS BOOK TO ALL OF THE TRUE WARRIORS who devoted their lives for the cause of Christ, giving us a testimony of His faithfulness and power! Some of them are with us still, and some have joined that great cloud of witnesses and are cheering us on! I honor and am so grateful for all who have taken their place on the timeline of history and passed to us the experiential knowledge of our spiritual inheritance.

Acknowledgements

To all of my friends and family, thank you for your love, prayers, support, and constant encouragement. I am so thankful to God for putting each one of you in my life! I love you dearly!

To those who wrote an endorsement for this book, thank you! I treasure you and am honored to have your friendship and support!

To my assistant and friend, Darlene Lynch, thank you for the hours and hours you spent, assisting with proof-reading the book and for all the prayers you have prayed for me to be able to write it. Your knowledge of the Word of God and your devotion to Him in everything you do is a great inspiration to me and to all who know you! You are greatly appreciated!

To Pastor Kim Owens, thank you for writing the foreword for this book. Thank you for taking your place as a true warrior, carrying the mantle of revival with power and demonstration to "leave the next generation a reference point." I honor you, my friend!

To Jim and Jacqueline Bryson at Spring Mill Publishing, thank you for your kindness, shared wisdom, encouragement, and help throughout the process of writing this book. Thank you for working with me to get this book published so quickly! I so appreciate you both!

To David Munoz, thank you for creating such a beautiful and anointed cover for this book! You moved at lightning speed to get it done, and you did an amazing job! I am very grateful.

Most of all, I thank God for loving me and for trusting me with these dreams, visions, and prophetic words. To You, O, God, be all the Glory!

Foreword

BECAUSE I STAND ON BROAD SHOULDERS of Pentecostal parents and grandparents who left a strong legacy and blazed a spiritual trail of passion and hunger for revival, I am excited and honored to be a voice to introduce Gina Gholston's new book, *Carry On*.

I met Gina at a conference in 2021, where she briefly introduced herself and proceeded to tell me that she'd had a significant dream with me and my husband in it. She asked if I'd like to hear it, and I said a resounding, "Yes!" That dream, *The Mantle of Revival,* is contained in the pages of this book and has marked my life and our church as we carry the assignment of sustained revival to our nation now almost eight years and counting. Gina's sensitivity to the Holy Spirit had her share this dream at such a strategic point in the revival and has been an ongoing source of the reality of the mantle and encouragement to wear it well for the sake of generations to come. I often say as the Lord spoke to me, "Kim, I want you to believe for a nation-shaking, history-making revival so that the next generation will have a reference point!"

You are holding in your hands a valuable resource to encourage, direct, and challenge you to be intentional about *your* mantle and assignment and to keep moving forward into *your* spiritual inheritance. Gina paints a masterpiece of the power of generational spiritual inheritance and our responsibility to steward it. Through her revelation of the Word of God, coupled

1

with her prophetic insight and vivid dreams and visions, Gina provokes us to look back and see not only who is watching and following us, but what kind of a spiritual trail are we blazing for them? The responsibility is on our shoulders now. There's a great cloud of witnesses watching and cheering us on. I love how she says that she heard the Lord say, "You will dip your pen in the ink of past movements…Then through you, I will continue to write the story."

I want to emphasize how much you will be equipped to believe for more than your current experience and spiritual level. You will want to enlist as a laborer for our generation's move of God.

As you read may you be gripped with all that it takes to *Carry On* what has been passed to us by the Early Church and those who blazed a trail of Pentecost and revival. It's our turn now! The best is yet to come.

Thank you, Gina, for reminding us of the value and substance of our spiritual inheritance, our access into the fullness of God.

Kim Owens, Revivalist
Pastor, Fresh Start Church Peoria, Arizona
Author, *Doorkeepers of Revival, Just to Make Religion Mad*

Introduction

THE THEME THAT YOU WILL FIND WOVEN through the chapters of this book is that we have a spiritual inheritance that is real and exceedingly powerful. Christ revealed the evidence of this inheritance through the pattern of His life and living as He walked on this earth. After His death, burial, and resurrection, He appeared to His disciples and told them to go to Jerusalem and wait for the promise of Holy Spirit to come upon them and into them, enduing them with "power from on high" (see Luke 29:49). After many days, Jesus then ascended into Heaven, and He sent back Holy Spirit. The Spirit which was in Jesus and enabled Him to walk in the power, wisdom, and likeness of God was the same Spirit that was given by promise of the Father to the Church in that upper room experience on the day of Pentecost. The Spirit of God came upon them and occupied their human bodies. He empowered them to take on the likeness of Christ. They taught with the same anointing with which He taught. They performed miracles, signs, and wonders by the same power that worked through Him.

The Church was birthed out of that encounter. This was God's original intention! He did not leave us comfortless! He left us empowered with His own Spirit to live our lives in the reality of the effects of our spiritual inheritance! It is an inheritance that never fades away (see 1 Peter 1:4).

Through salvation in Jesus Christ, we have been given access to this rich heritage. The breath of His Spirit now dwells in us, and His purposes must continue through us. Those who have gone before us paid the price to pass along the evidence of this inheritance. Laying their reputations—and even their very lives—on the line, they determined to obey God in order to give future generations knowledge of His power and evidence of His presence with us. We are inspired by the glory stories that we read and hear that came as a result of their devotion to the Lord, but it's not enough just to be inspired! Accompanying the inspiration must be a revelation of the undeniable responsibility that we now have. In order for the next generation to know and receive the spiritual inheritance that belongs to the children of God, we, too, must embrace and fulfill our part so that His fire continues to burn in us, no matter the cost.

It is my sincere prayer that this book will be an inspiration to each reader, a spark that ignites a flame in your heart and provokes in you a realization that you have a place in God's plan. If you have received Jesus as your Savior, the likeness of your Heavenly Father dwells in you by His Spirit. If you have not received Jesus as your Savior, I pray that you will. He's calling you. You are incomplete without Him. Without Him, we can do nothing, but with Him, we can become like Him and be empowered to be a conduit through which He can make Himself known.

Through the following pages, you will read dreams, visions, insights, and prophetic words that reveal the necessity for each of us to take our place in the plan of God. We must understand and deeply appreciate the value and weightiness of what we have been given—not in order to repeat what others have already done, but so that we can continue to build on the foundation that has been laid. May we be faithful stewards of that which we have received so that we leave behind the irrefutable evidence of God's power and glory to the degree that it ignites a passion in the next generation to receive and *carry on* with this spiritual inheritance.

1

Our Spiritual Inheritance

In Him [Christ] also we have obtained an inheritance, being predestined according to the purpose of Him who works all things according to the counsel of His will.

Ephesians 1:11 NKJV

I HAVE SPENT SOME TIME RESEARCHING my genealogical history. In my research, I found some very interesting stories and information about many within our family tree. There were connections to some historically famous people and also to several ethnicities that we never even knew about. I was even able to find pictures of some of my ancestors. It was exciting to look at those old photos and to realize that I have a connection with those people. I was amazed to see the genetic similarities that have been passed along through our family line. I remember seeing a picture of one of my grandpa's sisters. Sometimes, when researching genealogy, you can't be entirely certain if the information that you find really belongs to your family history, but when I saw that picture, there was absolutely no doubt that this was my ancestor because my mom looks almost exactly like her! It's amazing to make these precious discoveries.

Family has always mattered to God. It was His idea from the foundation of the world to have a family. He started the concept in the Garden of Eden when He formed man. He created this man in His own likeness. Think about that: the character traits of God as Father, placed in the genetic makeup of this human being! God wanted a representation of Himself in the earth realm, so He took the dust of the ground and breathed His breath into this man, thus creating all mankind with the potential to carry on the lineage of His likeness. Amazing!

Beginning in Genesis and all throughout the Old Testament, we read of the progression of this family, which eventually became a nation that God chose to be a people for His own. He started this nation with a man, whom He enabled to bring forth a promised son in his old age (see Genesis 21:2). That son begat another son, who begat twelve sons, who became twelve tribes. It's a remarkable history that reveals the unfolding of God's plan.

It was from this family that became a nation that we find the lineage of Jesus Christ (read Matthew 1:1-16). From the beginning of time, God has always had a plan to make Himself known to the world, and He does that through His people. The Old Testament reveals to us the faithfulness and demonstrated ability of God as He led and worked through His people, Israel. Through them, He revealed the evidence of His presence, and other nations were made aware of His unmatched power. As we move over into the New Testament, we see the display of the likeness of God—His power, attributes, and glory—continuing through the life of Jesus Christ during His earthly ministry. These recorded events were not just the makings of future Sunday School stories and good sermon material. His life and living were, and remain to be, the model that reveals to us the intentions of God for our own lives.

Jesus came to build the Church and establish a people who would be set apart as a royal priesthood and a holy nation unto God (see 1 Peter 2:9-10). This royal priesthood and holy nation would be comprised of those who accept Jesus into their lives as Savior and Lord. In so doing, they become members of His Body. According to Ephesians 1:22-23 and Colossians 1:18, Christ is the Head, and the Church is His Body. As His Body, we are the recipients of the inheritance that He came to reveal. Through our acceptance of Christ as Savior, we are born into the family of God.

> *For through Him we both [Jews and Gentiles] have access by one Spirit unto the Father. Now therefore you are no more strangers and foreigners, but fellow-citizens with the saints, and members of the household of God.*

> Ephesians 2:18-19 NKJV

The word household here is the Greek word *oikeios*, which means "a relative." The Apostle Paul further solidifies this statement:

> *The Spirit Himself testifies and confirms together with our spirit [assuring us] that we [believers] are the children of God. And if [we are His] children, [then we are His] heirs also: heirs of God and fellow heirs with Christ [sharing His spiritual blessing and inheritance].*

> Romans 8:16-17 AMP

In that same chapter, Paul also adds that those, who allow and devote themselves to be led by the Spirit of God, "are the sons of God" (see Romans 8:14).

Contrary to what some may believe, salvation is not just about getting us to Heaven; salvation is about getting us to God so that we can be positioned, as His children, to carry out His purposes to fulfill His original intentions in the earth. Through Christ, we, who were "in the world without God and without hope" and were once "far off" from Him, have now "been brought near" and have been grafted into the family of God (see Ephesians 2:12-13).

Being filled with the breath of His Spirit, Yeshua would empower the Church to then carry on His likeness in this earth realm. As born-again believers, the unmistakable markings of the family genetics now reside and continue in us.

Jesus is our pattern. He is not only our Savior, but He is also the model of what we are to become as members of His body. Showing us by example the power that is available to us by the inward and outward working of Holy Spirit, He exemplified the likeness of the Father, and we are to imitate Him and follow His example. When we take Him as our pattern, eventually we will begin to be an expression of that pattern, insomuch that when the world looks at us, they will see an example, a true representation of Him. He desires that we become effective imitators of God, carrying on with the plan, which He established from the foundation of the world. In and of ourselves, we could never achieve such a goal, but as we submit to Him, His Spirit works through us and enables us to do just that!

The Power That Works in Us

What is this inheritance that we receive as members of His family? The psalmist said, *"Lord, You alone are my inheritance"* (Psalm 16:5 NLT). The fullness of God that we see demonstrated in the human life of Christ is our inheritance as born-again heirs. Jesus said that everything the Father had was His and that Holy Spirit would take what was His and impart it to us (see John 16:15). The inheritance with which we have been entrusted includes all that Jesus is and has, which is all that the Father is and has.

Jesus said,

Most assuredly, I say to you, he who believes in Me, the works that I do he will do also; and greater works *than these he will do because I go to My Father.*

John 14:12 NKJV

How is it possible for us to take on the likeness of Christ and do the works that He did, and *even greater works* than He did? We are given the answer to this question in John, chapter 17, where we read that Jesus gave to us the same glory that He was clothed in. Acts, chapter 2, further reveals that He fills us with the Holy Ghost.

The birth of the Church came through the matrix of a powerful encounter with the resurrected Jesus on the day of Pentecost, as recorded in the Book of Acts. For those who obeyed and tarried there, that encounter was more than just a momentary touch from God; it was the reception of a *spiritual* inheritance that would impact their lives and times in profound ways. In that initial outpouring, 120 men and women were powerfully baptized by fire and filled with the Spirit of God, Himself. By His Spirit, He enabled them to become vessels through which the whole known world would be turned upside down with the reality of Him and of His resurrected Christ as He revealed Himself through them with the manifestation of undeniable miracles, signs, and wonders!

This is a picture of our spiritual inheritance, and it was not just for the early Church, alone. It is a treasure that is intended by God to be received by and to continue on through, every born-again believer from generation to generation.

The same Spirit that empowered Jesus in His ministry is the same Spirit that now abides in us. Now, it is no longer one man walking in the power of God, but a Body of many members, who carry the likeness of His person to every part of the world. The knowledge of the glory of God can now cover the earth as the waters cover the sea as this sold-out company, clothed in His glory and filled with His Spirit, moves effectively as His representatives.

From a family came a nation, from a nation came Messiah, and from Messiah came the Holy Spirit, Who enables us to walk in the power and demonstrated glory to reflect the very nature and likeness of Christ to a dark world and to lead those in darkness to Him. As Ms. Billye Brim so often says, "O, what a plan! And O, what a Planner!"

Our Divine Portion

The word *inheritance* means "to come into possession of or receive, especially as a right or divine portion" (Miriam Webster Dictionary). Those who pass down an inheritance do so with the intention of giving provision and resources to their beneficiaries. It is also a testament of their love and desire for their heirs to know and enjoy the benefits of that which they stewarded and received in their lifetime. Such inheritances can be life-changing for the recipients.

Heirs are legally entitled to receive the full portion of all that has been left to them. However, a key understanding to be pointed out is that when an inheritance is bequeathed, though the heir has full, legal access to its content, still, it must be received. In some instances, beneficiaries fail to claim their portion or don't even know they are entitled to an inheritance. What a sad situation!

It has been said that "what you don't know won't hurt you," but where our spiritual inheritance is concerned, a lack of knowledge has the ability to destroy us (see Hosea 4:6). We find an example of this very thing in the Book of Exodus. Some in

Moses' day doubted their inheritance and failed to occupy their divine portion. The inheritance was theirs by promise, but a wrong focus caused them to disregard the enabling power of God that accompanied the promise, and they died in a barren wilderness, instead of occupying the productive land that was intended by God to be their home.

As those who have been left with a great spiritual inheritance, we must not be ignorant of what belongs to us as the heirs of our Father, God. We must be diligent to know the Word of God which gives us revelation of all that He has made available to us. We must also remain steadfast in our focus on Him and in our obedience to Him so that we receive and experience the full benefits of that which He has given. Reception of our portion enables us to exhibit a true reflection of Christ's likeness and to continue to pass the knowledge and evidence of this inheritance on to future generations.

Jesus has promised that we can and should be filled with His Spirit and walk in the same power in which He walked to fulfill God's intended purposes for us as His Ekklesia. This flow of the transforming power of Holy Spirit's working through us enables us to reveal the effects and reality of our inheritance as believers. This promise is to us and for us, but we must be willing and obedient to believe it, receive it, and demonstrate it effectively so that the knowledge of its value isn't squandered, neglected, or diminished by our generation. We must represent Him well in our times.

Our First Priority

More than being a conduit for His power to be revealed, our first and foremost priority should be to cultivate and tend to our own personal relationship with the Lord. Spending time in His presence should be our greatest desire. As we allow the deep in us to receive what is pouring from the deep in Him, our hearts are knit together as one with Him. Jesus prayed for us to have this. As the Father was in Him, and He in the Father, He prayed that we would be one with Them. Without Him, we can do nothing. *Nothing!* It is in Him that we live and move and have our very being. So, we do not seek Him for just what He can do through us or for us, we seek Him first to know Him and to find our life in Him! To become one with Him, to love Him, and to know Him is the most necessary thing.

God invites us to draw near to Him, and in doing so, He will draw near to us (see James 4:8). This is His promise, and in His abiding presence, we become alive. Through salvation in Christ, we have been given full access to God. That is more important than any other thing.

When our time with Him, in worship, in prayer and communication, and just to sit in His presence becomes our first priority, everything then that flows out through us originates from the Source and becomes a river that brings life everywhere it goes! So, we must make time for Him in our daily routines. Allow Him to search us and know us! We must listen in prayer and become familiar with His voice so that we can recognize that inner witness as He leads us. Carry on! Keep being filled with His Spirit. Keep discovering Him. There are so many facets to God, and though we will never be able to comprehend all that He is, we can seek Him and find Him when we seek Him with our whole hearts. Never become so familiar with the idea of God that you fail to really know Him.

He is our God! He is great, and He is greatly to be praised! He is holy, but He is also approachable, and as we come into His presence with honor, reverence, and awe, we discover Him and are made aware of His greatness and goodness to us! Our personal pursuit, in itself, becomes a witness to all who are around us. Our attendance to our personal relationship with

Jesus gives Him access to deal with any and all things that would hinder His light, which allows His glory to shine even brighter and truer through us for all to see Him—Christ in us, the hope of glory!

The Realm of God

The ultimate portion of our inheritance is "reserved in Heaven for us" (see 1 Peter 1:3-4), but by the power of the Holy Spirit, we are enabled to manifest Heaven on earth. Jesus said to pray,

Our Father in Heaven, hallowed be Your name. Your Kingdom come. Your will be done on earth as it is in Heaven.

Matthew 6:9-10 NKJV

The word *Kingdom* here is concretely translated to mean "realm" (Strong's Concordance G932). So, "Your Kingdom" is referring to the realm of God. God's realm is the place where God dwells. It's His domain, and Jesus teaches us, in this passage, to pray expectantly that the power that abides in that realm where God dwells will manifest in this realm!

This is made possible when we are baptized in the Holy Spirit, Who is the promise and the "earnest of our inheritance" (Ephesians 1:13-14 KJV). The word *earnest* is a term for "a pledge or a first installment of money or property that is given *in advance* as security and assurance that the full amount will eventually be paid." In essence, Paul was saying that the Holy Spirit, Who was sent to us from the realm of God, is given to us as a promise from God—an *earnest* in our hearts—assuring us that the realm of God is real and ultimately will be revealed to us in its fullness. But until the fullness comes, Holy Spirit will manifest portions of what is happening in the realm of God to allow us to experience it here in the earth realm. He desires to, and can, manifest through us the reality of Heaven by displaying in powerful and demonstrative ways, evidence, and first-hand experience of the glory that comes from there.

Paul said in 2 Corinthians 3:18:

But we all, with unveiled face, beholding as in a mirror the glory of the Lord, are being transformed into the same image from glory to glory, just as by the Spirit of the Lord.

God's glory is His manifested presence, and He desires to have a dwelling place in this earth. In the Old Testament, God's glory dwelled in a man-made tabernacle. But, now, born-again believers become the house in which He abides. *"Do you not know that you are the temple of God and that the Spirit of God dwells in you"* (1 Corinthians 3:16 *NKJV*)? We are God's house, His temple. The temple of God in the earth is no longer a fixed structure built by man. He has chosen to tabernacle with us by the infilling of Holy Spirit, and through us, He desires to manifest the power of His glory. By the indwelling Spirit of God, we are transformed from our earthly glory and given the ability to experience and become a reflection of His divine glory—His nature and His likeness.

When those 120 men and women we read about in Acts 2 experienced and were baptized with the Holy Ghost and the fire of God in the upper room on the day of Pentecost, they were instantly transformed into witnesses, carrying the fire and glory of God. They were changed, and they knew it! They did not leave that room the same way they went into that room. They were still human beings, yes, but now they were human beings, housing the Spirit of God. And they did not take that lightly. They didn't just go back to living "normal" lives; they emerged from that place boldly carrying power that impacted the whole known world. They became living displays of the demonstrated power of God, giving everyone around them a taste of the realm of God. Their preaching was fervent and anointed with glory. Miracles, signs, and wonders were done by their hands as Jesus reached through them to reveal Himself to the world around them. They were given wisdom and ability that was so supernatural that it caused those around them to marvel and know without doubt that they had "been with Jesus" (see Acts 4:13). The whole book of Acts is a demonstration of the realm of God being revealed through the lives of submitted believers in Christ. Through them, we see the prayer of Jesus, "Your Kingdom come," become a reality. This is God's desire for all who are saved.

Those early Christians were no different than Christians today. They received the same Spirit that we receive when we are baptized with the Holy Ghost. As they were, so we can be also: carriers of God's glory! We look like Jesus, Who was and is the express image of our Heavenly Father. Through us, the world can see His likeness, His characteristics. This is our divine portion as "heirs with God and joint-heirs with Christ."

We cannot achieve this likeness on our own. That is why He sent us His Spirit, so that with Him and by Him, we have the ability to walk in demonstration of His power and presence, providing evidence of our received inheritance.

Though the purposes of those who have lived before us have been fulfilled, that doesn't mean that what they did is now insignificant and unworthy of our attention. To the contrary, Jesus said, that we are "entering in to their labors" (see John 4:38). They did their part for their time, and now we must pick up where they left off and continue it by doing our part for our time. The baton of what God ignited in the early Church and blazed through the lives of our ancestors is now in our hands, and we must choose to *carry on* with His purposes.

This inheritance is a treasure that is extremely valuable. It cannot be substituted and must never be neglected. It is life and death for this generation that is parched and desperate for a spiritual awakening. Many in the Church are groping in the darkness, living with constant hopelessness because they don't realize the value of all they have inherited as the children of God. They know what Jesus saved them *from*, but they know little about what He saved them *to*. Jesus' victory on the cross—His death, burial, resurrection, and ascension back into Heaven— released to us this remarkable spiritual inheritance. It's not just about something we receive when we all get to Heaven, but it's a right to our divine portion that becomes instantly available to us here and now. A lack of knowledge of that inheritance leaves many going through the motions but never coming to the full understanding of the truth. We are not victims of unchangeable circumstances. Through Christ, His Ekklesia is a triumphant, overcoming Body, against whom "the gates of hell cannot prevail" (Matthew 16:18).

If we fail to understand and invest this valuable inheritance that we have been given, then the benefits and reality of the power of God and the weightiness of His manifested glory are hidden from those who are in darkness. Christ is the Light, and He has placed that light inside us by the Spirit, and we must allow His light to shine (see 2 Corinthians 4:3-7). When we allow Holy Spirit to reveal the glory of God through us, those in darkness see the Light and are drawn to Him. *Demonstrated evidence of the glory of God is what sparks an awakening of an awareness of God that can come no other way!*

Imagine the Bible with no demonstrations of the glory of God—no record of the wonder-working power of God, no record of the Red Sea being parted, of David killing the giant, of Elisha raising the young boy back to life, or of Daniel being delivered from the lions den. Imagine having no record of Jesus opening blind eyes or raising Lazarus from the dead, or Himself being raised from the dead. Without the demonstration and manifestation of the glory of God, there would be no awareness of God, at all. There would be no gospel message, and you and I would still be in the world, without God and without hope!

Because ordinary people heard the gospel, believed in Christ, stewarded their relationship with Him, surrendered their lives to Him, and allowed themselves to become spiritual conduits through which the realm of God could be manifested in the earth realm, generations of people have been impacted and forever changed. The power of God flowing through their lives allowed the inheritance to be carried on generation after generation.

When those who follow us research the "family history," may they see such an unmistakable resemblance of our heavenly Father in us and in the story that we leave behind that they have no problem determining that God is real and that we really belonged to Him. May our part be fully completed so that our ceiling becomes their floor! May the spiritual inheritance be fully disclosed through our lives to such a degree that they will receive it, apply it, and carry on with the lineage of the Father's likeness!

Father, You have created us in Your image, and having accepted Jesus as Savior, we have been reborn into Your family. We are Your heirs! As Your very own people, may we fully exemplify Your likeness and the likeness of Your Son, Jesus. By our own might or power, we cannot accomplish such a calling. But by Your Spirit, we are enabled to live in the benefits and the reality of Your power so that the weightiness of Your manifested glory can be made known! Provoke within us a deeper revelation of all that You have made available to us so that we may walk in demonstration of Your power and presence. Stretch forth Your hand through us, Jesus, with miracles, signs, and wonders, providing undeniable evidence of our received spiritual inheritance. May Your light so shine through us that those around us will marvel and know that we have been with Jesus! We ask that Your glory would be revealed through us with such fervency and clarity that those around us can see an unmistakable resemblance of You, our heavenly Father. And seeing You in us, may they be drawn to a fervent desire to want to know You for themselves. May every person in Your Ekklesia become a spiritual conduit through which the realm of God can be manifested in the earth realm. May the reality of Jesus shine with such fervency that multitudes of people will be impacted and forever changed, allowing our spiritual inheritance to be carried on generation after generation, all for the glory of God. In the Name of Jesus, we pray! Amen!

2

We've Got Oil

Then He said to me, 'This [continuous supply of oil] is the word of the Lord to Zerubbabel [prince of Judah], saying, 'Not by might, nor by power, but by My Spirit [of Whom the oil is a symbol],' says the Lord of hosts.

Zechariah 4:6 AMP

I dreamed that my assistant, Darlene, and I were driving from Tennessee to a church in the northern part of Texas. I was going for a ministry assignment at this location.

As we were driving, I began to notice that beside *every* church that we passed was a tall, wooden structure standing over an oil well. These were like those wooden, tower-like structures situated over oil wells that you see in old movies.

We finally arrived at a small church and went inside to find a packed house. Every seat was filled, and people were even standing around the walls. On the platform, there were several people that I knew were pastors and church leaders. One of the pastors saw me, and he motioned for me to come to the front. So, we made our way to the platform, and I stood beside one of the church leaders, who had the microphone. He announced to the crowd, his voice quavering, "We are here tonight to pray for oil. America has such a deficit of oil, and we are crying out to God to give us oil. It's urgent, and we must join our voices and pray!"

After some time, we then went outside the building to the wooden, tower-like structure that was beside this church. All of the people inside the building came out with us, and when we got outside, an even larger crowd of people had gathered. There was a platform beside the structure, and all of the pastors and church leaders stepped up onto it. The same leader announced again to this crowd, "We are gathered here to pray for oil."

Finally, I just walked up and took the microphone, and I said, "But we *already* have oil! We just have to *release* it!" Some in the crowd, in agreement with what I said, began to shout, "Yes!"

At that time, several of us went and jumped into the deep hole in the ground beneath that wooden structure. When we did, a geyser of clear oil came bursting up. It was as if we, who knew we had oil, had jumped into that hole as a way to "prime the pump."

As the geyser burst forth, it launched us out of the hole, and we landed back on our feet. When we did, there were instantly several lines of people coming from all directions. There were thousands of people in those lines that stretched as far as the eye could see. In an instant, they had somehow heard that there was fresh oil, and they were coming from everywhere to get it.

There were some there who were bottling up the oil and giving it out to the people. They also had small handkerchiefs, like prayer cloths with the Appeal to Heaven flag on them, and they were soaking them in the oil and giving them out to the people.

I took the microphone and announced, "If you don't have oil, then get in and receive it. If you do have oil, then come and be refreshed, but go and release it to others!" As they came, we were "sending" them out from there to take the oil and release it everywhere they went.

End of dream.

Over the past few decades, we have found ourselves experiencing a lack of knowledge of our spiritual inheritance, which has left us with the reality of an extreme deficit of the manifested power of God in the Church. The focus of many began to be placed on soulish issues and attempts to be more culturally relevant, and they wandered farther and farther away from the original purposes of God, thus opening the door for darkness and deception to advance unchallenged. Now, the Church is being confronted with the realization that the lifeless form that has become the norm for those who have been lulled to sleep by the tones of a godless culture, has no power to deliver a nation and bring necessary change in the midst of a moral and spiritual crisis.

We have access to everything that we will ever need—exceeding, abundantly above all that we could ever ask or even think to imagine! Yet, being unaware of our abundant inheritance, many are given to anxiety, as though they are without hope. We gather to pray, but many of the prayers are prayed from a position of fear and uncertainty. A lack of knowledge of what we have inherited through Christ has left many crying out to God, asking Him to give us that which has already been given! Our situation is not hopeless! Power to bring change does exist. Hope is found in the revelation of Who Christ is and who we are in Him! Power is demonstrated through us as we understand that God is all-powerful and that all He is and has, has been extended to us as his heirs! We have oil! We just have to realize it, receive it, and release it by faith!

> *O, that we would receive the spirit of wisdom and revelation in the knowledge of God so that our eyes would be enlightened and we would see what is the expectation of His invitation and believe the valuable bestowment of the glory of His inheritance in the saints and the exceeding greatness of His power that resides in us who believe!*

Ephesians 1:17-18, paraphrased

There is more to our Christian walk than just attending church services and going through the ritualistic motions of our Sunday morning routines! God is real! Jesus is alive, and His fullness is available to all who will trust Him, believe Him, and avail their lives to Him. When your sincere prayer becomes "Lord, make me like You," He will then unlock the valuable bestowment of the glory of His inheritance in you, and out from you will flow rivers of living water, and the greatness of His power and nature will be seen!

Praise God, the awareness of our spiritual inheritance *is* being awakened in many within the Body of Christ. There is a company of enlightened believers that is jumping into the well of that inheritance to prime the pump so that the oil of refreshing and power can once again be released! And it's happening! The focus is shifting, and we are now beginning to witness another surge of glory.

One day I was reading 2 Chronicles 16:9 in The Living Bible translation. The scripture reads,

For the eyes of the Lord search back and forth across the whole earth, looking for people whose hearts are perfect toward Him, so that He can show His great power.

As I read this Scripture, it seemed that the words, "search back and forth," were being specifically highlighted to me. Then instantly, I saw a vision of a searchlight moving back and forth across the land. I asked the Lord what that was about, and I heard Him say, *"My searchlight is about to become a spotlight that will highlight those who have humbled themselves to walk with Me—not for their glory, but for My glory to be seen!"*

I am not saying that we are fully there yet, but more and more we are witnessing the return of the heirs, who are tired of living in spiritual poverty, and they are searching out the riches of their inheritance. More and more, we are beginning to see the fruit of that inheritance as God is highlighting those who have humbled themselves to walk with Him. And through them, He is revealing His glory. The geyser is erupting, and we are seeing the overflow as the oil of the Spirit is once again filling the Church and being spread through those who are not willing to stay uninformed, hidden, and helpless! Awakening has begun!

As I am writing this book, there is a fresh move of God that is beginning to be ignited in our nation. It began in a chapel service at Asbury University with a few students, who cried out to God for a true encounter with Jesus. They received that encounter and continued to fan the flames of revival with their worship and by surrendering their lives to the Lord. Word of this encounter quickly spread and ignited into a move of God that has now impacted thousands of lives as people from all across the nation, and even from other nations of the world, have begun to experience the transforming presence of the Lord for themselves. The flames of revival are now spreading to other college campuses, high schools, and churches. Even secular media is publicizing these God happenings. This is the beginning of a true, much needed spiritual awakening.

The wind of the Spirit is blowing again, and it is reigniting the fiery embers that have lain dormant for so long. Spiritual hunger is being stirred as many are witnessing the life-changing power of God touching so many, and the demonstration of His power and presence is provoking a relentless knowing that "there has got to be more, and we are fervently seeking God for it!" We cry out as did Habakkuk:

> *God, I've heard what our ancestors say about You, and I am stopped in my tracks, down on my knees. Do among us what You did among them. Work among us as you worked among them.*

> Habakkuk 3:2 MSG

The knowledge of our spiritual inheritance has awakened this spiritual hunger! We have tasted and seen the goodness of the Lord as the realm of God is once again being manifested by the awakened body of Christ. We are no longer content with the "weak and beggarly elements" that have been adapted and accepted by many as a "normal Christian walk." We HAVE oil, and we will no longer be satisfied with dry, dead religion. Our eyes have been opened, and our spirits have been reignited with this fervent pursuit. The well has been uncapped, and the flow cannot be contained. We are determined to receive the fullness of our spiritual inheritance with honor and in the fear of the Lord so that we experience it for our generation and pass it along to those yet to come.

The Follow-Through

The flow of the oil must never wane! The knowledge of its availability and unlimited power must never be withheld. We must not allow that to happen! Though it may seem a daunting, unachievable task, we must allow the move of God to continue. He NEVER meant for it to stop! He means for the river to widen, the fire to intensify, and the flow to become even greater! It's here! It's our time! We must jump in the well and allow the oil to flow freely through us once again!

Our "yes" to His invitation to receive and to carry on with this inheritance must be accompanied by a follow-through—meaning, our "yes" is not complete without our obedience to do all the Lord asks of us to do. It's not enough to just know about our divine portion. We must believe that God has made it available to us, receive it, and allow His power to be released through us. Obedience is a key that unlocks the door to the fullness of all that God desires to reveal. And our obedience must be given with the understanding that it is not by our might or power but that we must rely on the help and supervision of Holy Spirit. He imparts to us deep wisdom and understanding so that we can know and rightly function in the things that are freely given to us by God.

God's full purposes cannot be successfully accomplished by the intellect of men and mere words alone. There must be a submission to Holy Spirit on our part so that, in us and through us, He can demonstrate the realm of God and His manifested glory and power. Acts 5:32 states that God gives the Holy Ghost to those who will obey. The Lord declared that power is given to us when the Holy Ghost has come upon us and into us, and it is by His Spirit that we are enabled to release that power as effective witnesses for Him in the world (see Acts 1:8). So, the power is available—it is our inheritance—but it is our surrender and obedience to Christ that brings us into position to not only receive it but also to carry on with the work that He started.

Paul said that God *"is able to do exceeding, abundantly above all that we could ask or think, according to the power that works in us"* (Ephesians 3:20 emphasis mine). Notice the exceeding, abundantly that God is able to do is not according to our ability, it's according to the power that works in us. When our faith in God is activated by hearing and knowing the Word, Holy Spirit will then work with the Word to perform God's will in and through our lives.

So, it would stand to reason that in order for the power to work in us and through us, we must know the Word and be led by the Spirit. If we ignore the Bible, our faith in God will be weak. If we ignore Holy Spirit, we will be led by our own emotions and carnal nature, and though the power is available, it will not be fully operating in our lives! We have been given access to the fullness of God, and we must receive from Holy Spirit as He searches out the depths of this treasure and imparts it to us. In order to have the full operation of the exceeding, abundantly, above all that we can ask or think, we have to plug in to the power and allow it to work in us and be demonstrated through us.

We, the heirs, *are* awakening and taking our places on the timeline of God's plan. The realization of the valuable inheritance that we have received is causing a stirring within us that is reigniting an uncompromised pursuit for the restoration of what has been lost. It is provoking in us an undaunted resolve to see the power of God fully released to flow with even greater intensity and demonstration in our times. We are determined to have what belongs to us and to leave the next generation with more than just stories and the history of what God used to do. We are putting on Christ. We are being clothed in His likeness.

We are filled with His Spirit, and we will do our part in order that we might pass along the wealth of this spiritual fervency—not just with words that provoke an intellectual knowledge, but with demonstration that develops experiential knowledge of the Word and of the Spirit, which births confident faith in God.

As this remnant company arises, cloaked with the mantle of our spiritual inheritance and operating under the influence of Holy Spirit's guidance, the realm of God will be revealed and change will come. The geyser of an undeniable wave of transforming glory will be released! It's inevitable, and it will be unstoppable. I believe we have entered a time when the parched ground is about to be changed by the unblocked flow of the River of God's glory, and the power deficit is about to be recharged by a remnant company that carries the voltage of Holy Ghost potency.

As you continue reading, I pray you will do so with the understanding that we have entered a major moment with God. It is a moment in which He is making us aware of the value of what we have been given and of the urgent mandate that we have received from Him—to jump in and to release the oil of the Holy Spirit! We must give Him our committed "yes," receive His fullness, and carry on with the demonstration of our spiritual inheritance.

Father, through Christ we have been given access to everything that we will ever need—exceeding, abundantly above all that we could ever ask or think to imagine. All that You are and have has been extended to Your born-again heirs! As one of those heirs, I ask that You would grant to me the spirit of wisdom and revelation in the knowledge of You so that my eyes will be enlightened to the understanding of the valuable bestowment of the glory of Your inheritance that resides in me! Teach me to use the power that has been given to me by the Holy Spirit, Who now resides inside me! Saturate me afresh with the oil of Your Spirit! As the Wind of Your Spirit blows through this land, I hold out my ember and say, 'Reignite me, Lord! May I be a burning one for You!'

In this critical hour, may Your Church be ignited with a fresh fervency that provokes a vicious hunger for and passionate pursuit of You! May we all give You our uncompromised, 'Yes!' And may our 'yes' be accompanied by complete obedience that springs from complete trust in You! May our submission to You allow Your river to flow out of us with unavoidable waves of Your demonstrated glory to impact the world around us!

Your heirs are awakening, and we are putting on Christ! Clothed in His likeness, may all who see us, see Him! May our lives reveal Your power as Holy Spirit works through us, giving evidence of the reality of You and of Jesus, our righteous King and Savior! In His Name and unmatched authority, we pray! Amen!

3

The Mantle of Revival

But You, O LORD, are enthroned forever [ruling eternally as sovereign]; And [the fame and glory of] Your name [endures] to all generations.

Psalm 102:12 AMP

I ONCE READ AN ARTICLE THAT WAS WRITTEN about a man who had experienced a tragic accident that left him physically impaired and unable to continue working a job. As a result, he was financially reduced to living on a very minimal fixed monthly income. Although he lived in a debt-free home that he had inherited from his parents, still he was barely able to make ends meet, finding himself living in poverty.

One day he was watching a television program, which showed people bringing antique items to professional appraisers to discover their value. One guest on the show was a lady, who had brought with her an old blanket for appraisal. She was beyond shocked to find that her blanket was worth more than one million dollars! As the man was watching this, he suddenly remembered that, in his attic, was a blanket that looked exactly like the one that the lady was having appraised. The blanket had belonged to his great-grandmother, who knew its value and therefore had passed it on to her daughter—his grandmother.

However, his grandmother, over time, allowed the appreciation for this valuable treasure to fade from her memory.

Out of sight, out of mind.

Because his grandmother had little understanding of and appreciation for its real value, she had passed the blanket along to her daughter as nothing more than a sentimental family heirloom. All the man knew about the blanket was that his mother had used it to swaddle newborn kittens and then had casually stored it away in a trunk in the attic. There it had remained until a dire need had arisen and the memory of its existence had been stirred.

Curious as to whether or not this *was* the same type of blanket that he had seen on the television show, the man retrieved it from the attic and took it to be appraised. It turned out that his unappreciated, tucked-away item was actually a hidden treasure! It was a very rare Native American blanket that had been hand-dyed and hand-woven in the mid-1800s, and by *this* time, it was worth over two million dollars! This rich inheritance, which had been honored and greatly appreciated by his great-grandmother, had, over time, been left tucked away in the dark confines of a dusty old trunk, leaving a future heir with no awareness of what he had been given. He had been needlessly living in a state of poverty all because he did not know the value of the inheritance that had been handed down to him.

I'm sure you've already realized the reason I am sharing this story with you. It is a practical demonstration that sheds light on our current spiritual situation. The diminishing awareness and untapped resource of our rich spiritual inheritance have created a severe spiritual and moral decline in the Church and in our nation. The once thriving Church that we have read about in the Book of Acts has changed dramatically through the years.

There *are* points throughout the history of the Church, where we find resurgences of the power and operation of Holy Spirit, as some would search the Scriptures and find the recorded evidence of God's original intentions for the Body of Christ, and great awakening would come. Overwhelmed by the awareness of their spiritual inheritance, they would devote themselves to God, and through them, the flow of that power would continue. Rivers of life would come rushing through those seekers as God worked through them to transform the culture with waves of awakening revival. The more they sought Him, the more they experienced the reality of His glory and passed along the knowledge of their priceless inheritance to the generation that followed them, allowing them to experience it for themselves.

But then, there are other times in which some generations did not appreciate the inheritance, and they failed to pass along knowledge of its value. History shows that the effects of this not only impacted the Church, but with no visual and operational spiritual compass, the nation would also spiral into spiritual poverty.

Even in our lifetime, we have witnessed a decline in the experiential knowledge of God's original purposes for the Church. In recent decades, Holy Spirit has been depicted as merely a means to a prayer language or just an occasional touch of the emotions in a church service. Many within the Body of Christ became content to just go through ritualistic motions that were unaccompanied by the demonstration and power of the Spirit. This caused our rich heritage to be hidden away, creating a lack of knowledge of the fullness of the transforming power and glory that we have access to as heirs with God and joint heirs with Christ.

Uncomfortable with the understanding that the Book of Acts was actually the demonstration of the expectation of God for all of the Church for all times, many shied away from their true inheritance in an effort to make the "religious experience" more palatable to the culture. Not wanting to stand out in society, some sought to conform to society by hiding the Light that they carried. Churches began to compromise their foundational roots, and in an attempt to draw a bigger crowd, many pushed Holy Spirit to the back room, neatly tucking away His operations so as not to "overwhelm" or "confuse" those who would visit.

Out of sight, out of mind.

As time went by, with little or no demonstration of power and of the Spirit, a lifeless, unappealing form—an incomplete picture of the fullness of what the Church was intended to be— is what we have passed along to the younger generations that have been raised in this environment. With only an intellectual expression of God and no real experiential knowledge of His power, they have been deprived of the much-needed awareness of the inheritance that they have in Christ. They have been left in a condition of spiritual poverty that has made them very susceptible to the crippling deceptions and snares of a vicious adversary, who seeks to steal, kill, and destroy their lives.

Today, we find ourselves in a dire, seemingly hopeless situation in which darkness is covering the earth, and gross darkness, the people. Spiritual poverty has become acceptable but unnecessary because we have an inheritance that can change everything! It's time for the Church to be shaken to an awareness of God that provokes us to feel and hear His voice declaring:

"I LEFT YOU AN INHERITANCE!"

I believe that like Sampson of old, many within the Church are realizing that something is missing! We have become shockingly aware that the evidence of the full presence of Holy

Spirit is no longer among us, and there is a hunger to see that changed! An awareness of the richness of our inheritance has been remembered, and there is a "turning back to God" with a fervent passion that will no longer allow us to settle for less than what we have been given! Curiosity has overcome our complacency, and we are seeking God to know who we are in Christ and what we have access to as His heirs! We know there is more, and we are ready to discover the magnitude of our inheritance and allow the river to flow once again into us and out through us to the world around us! We know and are convinced that as we experience the fullness of what God has made available to us—by the Word AND by the Spirit—life will come, and undeniable change will happen!

The operation and supervision of Holy Spirit is not something the Church should avoid and dismiss but rather a necessity that we should embrace and welcome! Without His presence and involvement in who we are and what we do, we are powerless to be effective witnesses for Christ.

Two Dreams

The Lord gave to me two dreams that I believe will help us to see with greater clarity the reality of all that has been conveyed in this book so far. They also reveal with greater persuasion the call that we have received from the Lord to carry on with the treasure that we have inherited as His Church.

Dutch Sheets sometimes jokes that I have started dreaming in sequels. It does seem a bit odd, but it's actually a very important indication for us to consider. In the Book of Genesis, Joseph stated to Pharoah that when God gives "sequel" dreams, it is "because the thing is established by God, and God will shortly bring it to pass" (Genesis 41:32 KJV). A look at this passage in a couple of other translations of the Bible makes this even clearer to us. The New Living Translation reads:

As for having two similar dreams, it means that these events have been decreed by God, and He will soon make them happen.

The Amplified Version states:

That the dream was repeated twice to Pharaoh [and in two different ways] indicates that this matter is fully determined and established by God, and God will bring it to pass very quickly.

Much of the time prophetic words or dreams are given for a time yet to come, but the fact that God has given the following two dreams to me concerning His desire for the Church to continue with the flow and function of His original intentions is an undeniable indicator that something major is ready *now* to be revealed. Not only is it undeniable, it is established by God, and He intends to bring it to pass very quickly. So, it's time to put ourselves in the storyline and carry on.

The Mantle of Revival

The first of these two "sequel" dreams came to me on July 5, 2021. I actually closed the final chapter of my previous book, *Dreams of Awakening*, with this dream. I am sharing it again because it gives context for its sequel dream that I will later share.

This was one of the most profound dreams concerning revival that I have ever been given. It has deeply stirred me. To this day, I cannot read it or tell it without weeping—not with sadness, but with holy awe and in the fear of the Lord. O, His heart is that all people would know Him! How will they know unless they see Him in us and are told about Him? How will they see His mighty acts and hear of His saving power unless the Church is awakened to the reality of our calling to know and carry the Fire of God and to allow Holy Spirit to reveal the fullness of Christ through us?

In this dream, I was with a group of people—a total of eleven of us, including Pastors Paul and Kim Owens, and Larry Sparks, among others. We had been given the opportunity to visit a place that had great significance in revival history. We arrived at an old church that was built of a grayish-white stone. We stepped inside the church, and we noticed the wooden floors. I could hear our footsteps as we moved into the sanctuary. We looked around us. The ceilings were high, there was a balcony surrounding the sanctuary, and there was a high platform with a very large pulpit situated in the center of it. We were just walking around slowly, taking everything in and whispering among ourselves about how honored we all were to have been given this amazing opportunity to be in this place, to step on these floors, and to be in this atmosphere that was part of revival history.

We had initially thought we were alone in this sanctuary, but we began to hear a man's voice ringing out from behind the pulpit. Although, as the *people* in this dream we could not yet see the man, as the *dreamer* of this dream, I could see that he was on his knees with his right hand lifted toward Heaven, and he was in *deep*, travailing prayer. His prayer was so intense and full of passion and sincerity! As he prayed, it was as if he were being emptied out with every word. As he would speak, he would just slowly rock back and forth on his knees, with his hand lifted the whole time. His face was red because of the extreme intensity of his prayer. Probably four or five times, he repeated this same prayer:

"Alas, this *cross* that I must bear, 'tis not a *task* for me. Its *weight is light*, for my *delight* is to do *all* that You ask of me! I'm turning now to see *Your* face; 'tis *all* that matters to me! *I lift mine eyes. LORD, hear my cry: SHOW ME YOUR GLORY?*"

As he prayed these words over and over, it was as if an electrical current could be tangibly felt, and we were all brought to tears as the weightiness of the presence of God completely filled that room. Our group reverently walked to our left and sat down on a pew, not wanting to disturb the man, who was praying.

I don't have words to really explain this, but the whole atmosphere just *filled* with the pleasure of God. I wish I were able to articulate that! We could feel that God was *so pleased* with this man and with this prayer. The feeling of God's pleasure was real and almost tangible. Again, I don't know how to adequately describe that.

As he continued to pray, I was sobbing, overcome by the presence of the Lord. The rest of the group did the same, and the man heard us. He got up off his knees and walked toward the pulpit. I noticed that he was a tall man. He was young, and he had on clothing that appeared to be from the early 1900s. The pulpit was very large, and there was a step behind it, and the man stepped up onto it. He then leaned over the pulpit and saw us there. With his elbows on the pulpit and his face resting in his hands, the man was gazing at us and said with deep emotion, almost in a whisper, "You *came!* You're *here!*"

He then stood up straight, and we saw that he was cloaked with what appeared to be some type of robe, but it wasn't natural clothing. Again, I find it hard to adequately articulate what we saw. The robe was very thick, bulky, and long, touching the floor. You could tell it was old and extremely heavy. He then said to us, "I have been waiting for you!" He put his hand on that robe, and he said, "I wore this for my time, and it was all that I desired! It was *all* that I desired!"

I was almost afraid to speak, but reverently I asked, "What is it?"

He answered with such respect for it, "It's the mantle of revival!"

I then asked, "Who are *you*?"

"That is not important. What *is* important is that you came to get this mantle. You have been sent here for this purpose."

We had thought we were there just to see that building, but we now understood that we had been deliberately, even supernaturally, brought there by God to receive that mantle. That realization was very overwhelming to each one of us.

The young man then began to tell us stories about that mantle—the story of how he had received it and stories of the experiences he had while carrying it in his time. We then realized this mantle was the "cross" he was so intently speaking about in his prayer. Though heavy, it had not been a burden for him; it was the greatest joy of his life!

As he spoke to us, we noticed that the mantle, which was still on him, was growing. It was extending with every word he spoke. It was filling up the stage. He said, "In my time, I cried out to God and asked for at least 100,000 souls to be touched and changed by the power of God, but in your time, it *must be much greater!*"

The mantle continued to grow, and he continued to speak. He was giving us instruction and revelation about this mantle because it was being passed to us so that we would carry it for *our* time.

As we listened in awe to all he was telling us, the realization hit us that we were going to carry that mantle, and we all just looked at each other with a look that said, "We can't *carry* that! It's too heavy! It's too big!" We were amazed that he was still able to stand under the weight of it as he spoke to us. I was so overcome by the magnitude of what was happening, and I was sobbing. I got up off the pew and stepped out into an aisle and just fell on my knees. Everyone else in the group did the same. Knowing that we had for certain been sent by God to receive this mantle, I asked the question that I, along with everyone else, was thinking: "How can we carry it? It's so BIG!" In the natural, it seemed impossible!

The man then said, "You cannot wear this mantle and look forward or around you. If you do, it will be torn and misused, and it will become cumbersome and even wearisome for you. You must *ever* look upward and be *completely* enthralled by the Lord. *Focus* on Him! *Pursue* Him! *Long* for Him, and soon the weight of the mantle will be absorbed by the passion in your heart for more of Him."

He then said with profound joy, "Now… it's *your* time to carry the mantle!"

In unison, still weeping, we said, "We receive it! We don't completely know how, but we receive it!" Then, out of the depths of our beings, we began to pray that same prayer the man had prayed at the beginning. It just rose up out of us. That prayer became the cry of each of our hearts. We prayed:

"Alas, this cross that I must bear, 'tis not a task for me. Its weight is light, for my delight is to do all that You ask of me! I'm turning now to see Your face; 'tis all that matters to me! I lift mine eyes. Lord, hear my cry: SHOW ME YOUR GLORY!"

The man stepped down from the step behind the pulpit, back onto the stage, and then he was just gone. (I believe the young man may have been Evan Roberts, a young man who was instrumental in the great Welsh revival that took place in the early 1900s.)

Still on our knees, releasing this intense prayer that had now become *our* prayer, that mantle was lifted from that stage and placed on us. It covered us and was now big enough to fill that entire church. As the mantle covered us, it then lifted us up and became like a hang glider of sorts and began to carry us. I could see water beneath us as we were being carried by the mantle over the ocean. Then we could see land, then mountains, and then we landed, facing westward. With the mantle still covering us, we all knew that we were in the mountains of North Carolina at the place where a Holy Spirit outpouring came upon a small group of men in the late 1800s and early 1900s that later launched the Church of God and the Church of God of Prophecy denominations. Out in front of us, in the span of about twenty feet in width, we saw large, white stones making

41

up letters that were each about four feet tall, which spelled the words, "TO BE CONTINUED."

That was the end of the dream.

Throughout history, there have been many powerful moves of God. It is so encouraging to look back at what God did in those times. We are inspired by the knowledge of what He has done, but we must never settle into the confining idea that He is finished! Those revivals serve as a witness to us that what God has done, He intends to do again—and even greater!

God has determined that "America shall be saved," and He has revealed that the salvation of this nation will come as the result of another great awakening. Many have felt and even prophesied that a third Great Awakening will be experienced around the world. The time has come when that prophesied awakening is now unfolding, and there is a clarion call echoing from the heart of God to the Church. It is the call to carry the mantle of revival so that His transforming glory can be manifested once again through us in *our* time.

The wind of revival is beginning to blow again, and there is a company of awakened warriors, who are arising with an understanding of our inheritance. We must not lose the fervency of the flame of Yah that is ours to carry! The move is on, and we must receive the mantle that has been passed to us.

This move of God we have entered into will not be about prestige and a few preachers gaining public recognition. Who we are is not important! Revival is not about our glory or our fame; revival is all about *Christ's* glory and *His* fame being made known to and through His Body. True revival provokes a gripping awareness of God as He works through those who are willing to "put on Christ" and become unavoidable lights shining in a dark world with the evidence of His abiding presence. True revival is

42

the result of glory revealed. The manifestation of the glory of God will not only affect the Church, it will extend far beyond our pulpits and church gatherings to impact lives, government, culture, and even the overall atmosphere of regions, states, the nation, and the world.

It's time, and we MUST show up for this moment! We must receive the mantle with honor and with the fear of the Lord and carry it for our generation and for the sake of those yet to come.

Carry On with the Mantle

I wasn't sure if the "TO BE CONTINUED" message that was displayed at the end of the dream was saying that I would have another dream or if it was stating that the outpouring that had been experienced in that particular location all those years ago must be continued. It turned out to be both.

Almost a year after having the first dream about the mantle, I received another dream from the Lord that "continued" where the first one left off.

On May 21, 2022, I dreamed that Pastors Paul and Kim Owens, my assistant, Darlene, a couple of other people (I don't remember who they were), and I were at Fields of the Wood near Murphy, North Carolina. We were sitting at a picnic table located near the gift shop. We were all facing outward, in the same direction, looking toward the parking area and the pond that is located there.

We had come to this place on a prayer assignment, and we were taking a moment to rest and reflect on the day. We were praying, "Lord, what do we do now?" As we prayed that, a car pulled into the parking lot and parked kind of close to where we were sitting. A few young people got out of that car and went scurrying off to the gift shop. Then the passenger door opened, and we could see an elderly lady getting out of the car. When she closed the door, we could see that she was so emaciated; she was just skin and bones. She was very weak and kind of bent over, and she could barely walk on her own, so I ran over to her to help her.

She said, "Thank you, honey."

I said to her, "Come and sit with us."

I then led her up to the picnic table where we were all sitting. She was dressed in very nice clothes, with a long-sleeved, jacket-type shirt, and I remember she had very thick, wool socks on her feet and no shoes. It was very hot that day, so I asked her if she was cold.

She said, almost in tears, "O, yes, I am really cold. I just can't seem to get warm."

I said, "Well, we've got this mantle, and if you'll sit down here, I'll cover you up. It's very heavy, so we can't put much of it on you because there's no way you could hold up under the entire weight of it, but we can wrap you up in the corner of it."

Kim and Darlene got up and helped me take a part of the mantle and wrap it around the lady. As soon as we did, she said, "Wow! What is this?"

Then the three of us just looked at each other as a revelation hit us, "It's the mantle of REVIV-ALL!"

I said to the lady, "This is the mantle of revival, and it revives."

She said, "I feel it! I feel it!"

We literally watched as, right before our eyes, strength and life came into that lady. Her body filled out, and she stood upright, completely restored and made whole.

She was smiling and glowing with peace and joy. We just sat with her, rejoicing in her miracle. Then after a while, she left, and we all just sat there, looking at each other in amazement, wondering, "What just happened?" We were just so shocked!

Then the Lord spoke audibly; we all heard His voice! He said, "I gave you the mantle; now I'm going to show you what to do with the mantle. It's not to be worn and talked about just for its beauty. There is purpose for the mantle, and there is purpose for My putting the mantle on you. You have to learn how to use it for My purposes. This is My answer to your question, 'what do we do now?' Now, you must learn how to *use* the mantle."

People then began coming to us. They would tell us of various problems, health issues, or situations they were dealing with, and we would sit them down at that table and wrap them in the corner of that mantle.

One young couple came, and they were weeping. They were having severe marital problems. We wrapped them in that corner of the mantle, and they were each healed and delivered of emotional issues, and their marriage was restored!

Another man came on crutches. He had had knee surgery, and something had gone wrong that permanently damaged his knee. We wrapped him in the mantle, and instantly, he was healed!

Some who came were sinners. They saw what was happening, and they just came up to ask us what was going on. We would tell them about Jesus and His power to heal, deliver, and save, and we would then wrap them in the mantle, and they would be gloriously saved and instantly baptized in the Holy Ghost! We could literally see a physical transformation as the joy of the Lord would just overtake their whole countenance.

Over and over the people would come. We only used the corner of the mantle because we knew the weight of it would be too much for any who was coming to us, but there was so much power in just the corner of it, that everyone who came supernaturally received what they had need of. And they would all rejoice and give glory to God.

Over and over, throughout the dream, God would speak to us audibly, saying, "This is the mantle of REVIVE-ALL. It's to revive. It's to make alive again It's to bring change. It's not for looks, and it's not for the exaltation of those who wear it. There's a purpose in My putting the mantle on you, and now I'm going to teach you how to use it for My purpose."

We were all so happy! We were rejoicing, looking at each other in complete amazement and excitement for all we were witnessing, and we knew this was only just getting started.

That was the end of the dream.

What an amazing and revealing dream! When I awoke from it, I was literally sobbing! It was so real that it was as if I had really been there! In this second dream, we were in the same location in which we had "landed" with the mantle at the end of the first dream. This was the place where we had seen the large, white stone letters forming the words, "To be Continued" I was just wrecked by the presence of God as I realized, *This is the continuation*. I was overcome with a deep sense that we are being launched into another great move of God in the days to come, and there was an urgency in my spirit that was provoking in me the need for us to grasp the understanding of how to effectively work with God in this move.

God is now teaching us the "next" thing, which is how to use the mantle to reveal His power. We are entering the time when the Church is going to operate in the full function of God's intentions. Evidence of Holy Spirit power is about to become a visible reality as the Lord works through us to make Himself known!

4

The Continuation

Therefore, we also, since we are surrounded by so great a cloud of witnesses, let us lay aside every weight, and the sin which so easily ensnares us, and let us run with endurance the race that is set before us.

Hebrews 12:1 NKJV

WHEN I CONSIDER THE DETERMINATION OF THOSE we read about in previous generations—how they encountered God and became gripped by Him and how that encounter changed the whole focus of their lives—I am provoked in my desire to know Him as they knew Him! I believe it is something deep inside our spiritual nature that identifies with their hunger to know the fullness of God. The seed of that same hunger has been planted inside each of us by our Creator. When the time comes for those seeds to be awakened, we are then left with a decision. We must choose either to pursue the fruit of God's intentions or to allow the seeds to lie dormant, their purpose unrealized. I once heard the Lord say:

> I Am releasing a flow of My power that will now awaken and commission My called-out ones, My for-such-a-time-as-this ones! It is not awakening as though they are asleep, but I will awaken that which I have

placed in them! I will now breathe on and activate the seeds of purpose that I have sown into this called-out company, and they will rise, and I will send them out with power and strategy to fulfill the purposes that have been awakened!

The time has come once again when the Lord is stirring our remembrance. He is awakening us to an awareness of the power that we have inherited as Spirit-filled believers. As in the dreams, we have been given access not only to explore and to be in awe of this "mantle" of power, but He has called us to receive the mantle and carry on with the purposes of God.

I find it very interesting that in the first "mantle" dream that I shared in the previous chapter, the Lord chose to highlight the great Welsh revival that took place in the early 1900s. What God did in that time was nothing short of amazing! Supernatural events revealed the power of God to such a degree that the entire nation was gripped with an awakening to an awareness of God.

In that revival, the young Evan Roberts was deeply stirred with an uncommon pursuit of God that was so intense and fervent that it overtook his whole life. Fully devoted to giving God what He wanted, which was a massive spiritual awakening in Wales, Roberts unknowingly became instrumental in sparking a fiery move of God that not only touched his nation, it eventually even spread around the world! It was a movement that continues, even now, to be a historical model that provokes spiritual hunger in thousands of lives. The dream revealed the passing of the mantle of that amazing move of God onto our shoulders. The passing of the mantle and the words written in the white stone letters that ended the first dream, I believe, were God's way of reminding us that what He started, He intends to be continued!

By highlighting this awakening revival in Wales, Holy Spirit is not telling us He will replicate exactly what happened in the Welsh awakening. Nor are we to seek Evan Roberts' mantle of revival. It is not Evan Roberts' mantle; Holy Spirit owns and dispenses mantles. We seek God, not people. Nor are we to try and duplicate or copy what Holy Spirit did in the past. We can, however, be inspired and instructed by it. And also, by honoring what Holy Spirit did then, as well as the efforts of those He used, we can drink from the same well of power and anointing. By using this revival as a picture of what He is about to do, God is saying to our generation, 'I Am about to bring forth an earth-shaking, nation-changing outpouring of My Holy Spirit. It will produce great deliverances, salvations, healings, and societal transformation.

(Dutch Sheets, Give Him 15, June 1, 2022)

Holiness People

Besides the Welsh revival, there was another spiritual movement that the Lord calls to our attention in both of these dreams. The location of that major Holy Ghost outpouring is known today as *The Fields of the Wood* near Murphy, North Carolina.

The movement started, at first, in the remote hills of east Tennessee in 1886 as a small group of men were gripped by Holy Spirit to go deeper in their revelation of Christ and His intentions for the Church. They began to regularly meet and pray in an old grist mill. Their study of the Book of Acts and the Pauline Epistles in the Bible brought about in them a definite knowing that, concerning the Scriptures, they had only seen in part. That revelation left them with an insatiable desire to understand more clearly what God wanted to do in and through their lives. Eventually, the number of seekers grew, and they moved to a schoolhouse just across the state line in Camp Creek, North Carolina. There, over one hundred people received the baptism of the Holy Ghost and spoke in tongues "as the Spirit gave them utterance." Miracles, signs, and wonders began to occur as word of the outpouring spread like wildfire through the mountains, drawing people from near and far to come and encounter the Lord.

My spiritual roots run very deep in this particular movement. My great-grandmother was a member of the foundational congregation that began to be formed from this outpouring. It was a powerful move of God that ultimately impacted the nation.

A vicious hunger for more of God was birthed and fervently burned in this group of people. That hunger caused them to experience the Holy Spirit on levels they had never experienced before, and it also enabled them to withstand great persecution that would unfold in the days and years that followed. The more they learned and experienced about the revelation of their spiritual inheritance, the more distant they became from the traditional "norms" that had been adapted and accepted by the Church at that time. Many around them were unwilling and afraid to believe there was more, and they began to severely persecute that remnant company in hopes of putting a stop to this new movement. But once the revelation was received and experienced by that remnant company of believers, there was no stopping their pursuit. They were determined to have and to do all that God wanted them to have and to do.

They came to be known at that time as "holiness" people. That term has taken on a lot of negative connotations through the years, most of which revolve around traditionalism and legalism that have actually held many in bondage to some of the very chains that those early pioneers paid so dearly to be freed from! However, "holiness," in its original meaning, has nothing to do with religion and everything to do with God's intentions for His people. The primary meaning of the word *holy* is to be sacred, set apart. God refers to Himself as being holy. He is incomparable, different from all others. There is no one or nothing like Him. He is set apart, and He calls us, as the Church, to be holy, set apart, as He is holy and set apart.

It is not our outward appearance or church affiliation that sets us apart. We are not holy because we hold to a plethora of man-made rules and doctrines. Jesus' living in and through us is what makes us different!

Paul says that we must "put on Christ" (see Romans 13:14). To put on Christ is to take on His likeness (see 2 Corinthians 3:18). To be clothed in His likeness is to become a living demonstration of the effects of His very nature and presence to the degree that those around us know, without doubt, that we belong to Him and that it is He Who is living and working through us by His Spirit. The closer we draw to Him through worship, consecration, spending time in the Word, and in personal fellowship with Him in prayer, the more we desire to be like Him. We put off the old man of sin, and we take on His attributes, His ways. And when we are filled with His Spirit, we are given access to His thoughts (read 1 Corinthians 2:9-16). As we think His thoughts, we become transformed by the renewing of our minds to know and to do the good, acceptable, and perfect will of God for our lives (see Romans 12:2). Then it is no longer we who live, but it is Christ Who lives in and through us, manifesting His love and power to the world around us.

In the Book of Exodus 33, we are given details of a conversation that Moses had with the Lord. In that conversation we find that Moses understood the concept that God's presence upon Israel is what "separated them"—set them apart—from all the other people upon the face of the earth (verse 16).

The early Church was so transformed by the power of God, that in Antioch, the people referred to them as Christians, followers of Christ (see Acts 11:26). They were set apart, different, and that difference marked them as unmistakable members of Christ's Body, the Church. Christ in us is the hope of the glory of God being revealed through us.

Paul said in 2 Corinthians 4:6-7 KJV:

For God, Who commanded the light to shine out of darkness, hath shined in our hearts, to give the light of the knowledge of the glory of God in the face of Jesus Christ. But we have **this treasure** *in earthen vessels,* **that the excellency of the power may be of God, and not of us** *(emphases mine).*

Our world is sliding down the slippery slope of godlessness. People MUST know Jesus! To know Him, they MUST "see" Him! Paul tells us in 2 Corinthians 4 that Christ is the Light, and through the new birth, God puts His Light in us! His Light shining through us and His righteousness seen upon us sets us apart from the world around us. That is not to say that we are better than any other. It's not about pride and elitism; it's about the transformation that is made when we accept Jesus as Lord of our lives. He delivers us out of darkness and fills us with His marvelous light. Now, we shine as lights in a dark world, pointing others to Him.

When those 20th Century pioneers were termed "holiness" people, at that time, it wasn't a reference to a religious legalism. It was a descriptive fact. It was undeniably obvious that something was different about them. Their encounter with the Lord and their experiences that came as a result of their continual pursuit of His presence had set them apart from what was considered to be the "normal" Christian experience. This is the very essence of true holiness. As one minister said, "The opposite of holy is normal." The more those men and women pursued a deeper revelation of Christ and His purpose for them as His Body, the more they experienced and radiated with the undeniable evidence of His abiding presence and the less "normal" they became.

Awakening had come, and like a massive river flowing, the current could not be avoided or stopped. The embers that had lain dormant for years had now been awakened, and the flames began to be revived and stoked into a visible fire of God's demonstrated power. Being "at ease in Zion" was no longer an option for those who had been awakened and revived. Their hearts now burned for Jesus—to know Him and to make Him known. The revelation of their spiritual inheritance became a catapult that launched them into an awakening to God that would be greater and more far-reaching than any of them could have ever imagined!

It is intriguing that this outpouring began in a millhouse at a place called Barney Creek on the outskirts of Tellico Plains, Tennessee and then moved to a schoolhouse and a log cabin in a place called Camp Creek, North Carolina. As more and more believers jumped into the River of God's outpouring, the "creeks" became a "river," and a wave of restoration power began to build!

For that small group of early pioneers, who gathered for days, and even years, to seek God and to ask Holy Spirit to open their eyes to true understanding of the Scriptures, revelation of that initial outpouring and movement that they had read about in the Book of Acts became more than just a Bible happening. For them, it became a provocation that led them to desire and experience the same encounter for themselves. They sought God, and He honored their sincere pursuit with another outpouring of Holy Ghost power. As heirs first learning of their priceless inheritance, they latched hold of what belonged to them, and the flames of that Pentecostal fire were reignited inside them, setting into motion another world-changing movement.

The movement that began in those mountains was ten years before the more well-known Azusa Street revival. The current that began to flow in the hills of Tennessee and North Carolina made its way into other states. It touched the lives of thousands of people and released a flood of revival all across America. The flood became a wave of glory that culminated in a crescendo of the manifested power of God in an old warehouse building at 312 Azusa Street in Los Angeles, California, which eventually impacted the world.

From the fire that was poured out on the day of Pentecost, the Church was launched and continued to grow as generations following became aware and active recipients of their spiritual inheritance. It was that same fire that continued to burn in Wales, in the early 20th Century outpouring in Tennessee and North Carolina, and in all of the other great moves of God throughout history. And it is still available for the Church today. Just as Holy Spirit empowered them to be like Jesus—to endure whatever they had to endure, and to reveal His power—He is also in us and will do the same for us.

The inheritance is now being revealed to the heirs of salvation in our time. Aware heirs are rising up with a fervency that is unmatched by any other generation because now the mantle has grown, and the weight of glory has increased. The urgency of the time has provoked a remembrance of and a desire for this valuable treasure that belongs to us as the children of

God, and we will not allow it to lie hidden, dormant, and unused while we just struggle through this life. *We have an inheritance*, and we must awaken to the realization that we have received a mandate from the Head of the Church to shine as lights pointing the world to Him. We must recognize the value of what we have been given and receive it with honor. As we learn to use the mantle, it continues to grow and intensify, enabling its effects to reach farther in scope as evidence of its reality is seen in us and passed on through us to multitudes around us...and even to those yet to come.

We must embrace the mantle and do our part for our time. No matter the cost, we must never stop!

A Rich Inheritance

Recently, I had the distinct honor of speaking at the home-going celebration of my 90-year-old aunt. Married for over seventy-two years and serving in pastoral ministry for several decades, she and her husband have been great role models for me all my life. I feel it would be fitting and appropriate to share with you the following portions of the tribute that I wrote and shared that day:

> I enjoy reading the account of the life of Joseph in the Bible. I am always inspired when I read of his unrelenting faithfulness to God. No matter what he faced, Joseph remained true to the Lord, and he found that, through it all, God was always with him, navigating his life to fulfill the destiny and purposes that He had for him. Joseph was devoted to God, and his decision to walk with the Lord didn't just affect his own life, but through him, many people were powerfully impacted. Even today his life impacts us, as we read his story.

One day, while reading his story, I received a revelation from the Lord, and I wrote these words: *The marking of a true warrior is not their battle scars, it's their sustainability! True warriors do not stop, and they are not driven by fear nor distracted by the memory of past battles. They are driven by righteous purposes and pursuit of the One their soul loves! They do have many scars, but they do not see themselves as victims, but as victorious and triumphant overcomers through Christ! True warriors are forerunners. Their focus is forward. Their passion is for the Christ, Whom they follow and imitate.*

As I read and remembered these words, I was deeply struck with a strong realization that we have been blessed to have many examples of true warriors in our lifetime—warriors like Joseph—who knew God and devoted their all to Him! They may not have known that they were warriors. They were just living their lives, but they lived their lives on purpose for Christ, thus blazing a trail for us to follow! It wasn't always easy for them—and they didn't hide that from us—but they trusted God and showed us by example that He is trustworthy. There was a steadfastness about them and an unhidden devotion to the Lord that impacted everything about their lives, and it shined a light that made us all aware of the difference that a true relationship with Him can make in our own lives. Their faith in God and their faithfulness to Him have given us the priceless knowledge of an available spiritual inheritance that is beyond description!

As I think about this, I am reminded of the following verses in Psalms:

"One generation shall praise Your works to another and shall declare Your mighty acts... Men shall speak of the might of

Your awesome acts and declare Your greatness. They shall utter the memory of Your great goodness and shall sing of Your righteousness... They shall speak of the glory of Your kingdom and talk of Your power, **to make known** *to the sons of men His mighty acts and the glorious majesty of His kingdom"* (Psalms 145:4, 6-7, 11-12 NKJV emphasis mine).

The true warriors, whom we have been so blessed to read about and even to personally know and to be impacted by, left us with a living witness of the faithfulness of God and His incomparable power! They willingly took their places on the timeline of history, and they pioneered movements of truth, power, and demonstration of the Spirit. The sacrifices they made and their fearless obedience to the leading of Holy Spirit allowed Heaven to invade the earth, and even to invade our very lives in powerful and undeniable ways. They left for us a solid foundation on which to build.

They shouted the message of the goodness of God and of the reality of Jesus to us. Now we must do the same for the generations that will follow us. It may not always be easy, but it won't always be hard, either, because our faith in God sustains us and enables us to see beyond the difficulties. We may have many scars, but we are not victims! We are victorious, triumphant overcomers through Christ! They taught us that!

Some of those warriors have now joined with that great cloud of witnesses, and they are there, cheering us on while we are here! I believe their challenge for all of us would be, "Run on, warriors! Run hard! It's your turn to be the light for others! Don't waste time! Go! Be the example! Run with undaunted obedience with your gaze set on Jesus so that the generations that follow you will not be deprived of the awareness of the great inheritance that is theirs through Christ Jesus!

The mantle is being extended to us. It's our turn to carry it, and the choice of whether or not we will receive it and run with it is up to us. But, run with it we must! The generations following us are dependent upon it! We are in a time like no other, and now more than ever before, there are those around us who need godly role models. They need spiritual mothers and fathers, who will unashamedly shine the light of Christ into the darkness and show them, by example, a more excellent way. May all who come behind us see in us the testimony of a true warrior. This is our gift to those who labored before us, and it is our highest calling in Christ, Who is the ultimate True Warrior.

Use the Power

So, what do we do now? Remember in the second "mantle" dream, the Lord answered that question: "I gave you the mantle; now I'm going to show you what to do with the mantle. It's not to be worn and talked about just for its beauty. There is purpose for the mantle, and there is purpose for My putting the mantle on you. You have to learn how to use it for My purposes. This is My answer to your question, 'what do we do now.' Now, you must learn how to use the mantle."

The power is available, and it is God's desire to work through us to "revive-all." He demonstrates His love through the revealing of His power. Lives are changed when they are confronted with the reality of almighty God working on their behalf.

We see a clear example of this in the third chapter of Acts when a crowd of people witnessed the lame man walking for the first time in His life. That miracle left no doubt that Jesus was indeed the Son of God. That visible evidence of the undeniable effects of the power of God, which was released through Peter and John, caused thousands to believe in Him and to be saved.

If you will allow me to paraphrase Peter's response in that historic moment, it may have been something like this: "Silver and gold is not what we have, and it's not what you need, but we do have this mantle, and we extend that to you!" Peter and John's encounter with God in the upper room had so permeated their being that His power now flowed out through them to give an introduction of Him to a group of people who thought they already knew Him and to a world that previously had no access to Him. That is the amazing truth of the inheritance that we have been given!

People are waiting, and even desperate, for the revealing of the reality of Jesus. O, they may say they don't believe in Him, and some may even mock the Church, but when the demonstration of His power and Person begins to be seen, curiosity will provoke hunger, and hunger will provoke pursuit. Pursuit will lead to revelation and encounter, and true revelation and encounter with God and His Christ will transform lives even the lives of those who previously had no desire to know Him!

I remember many years ago, when my nephew was about five years old, we were quietly driving down the road as he sat buckled in his booster seat in the back. Suddenly, he unbuckled himself, leaned up on the console, and made an announcement to us! It was as if he had been overtaken by a revelation and had become instantly anointed to release it, with my mom and me as his audience. "The problem with the Church," he said, "is they have the power, but they don't know how to use it!" Releasing these words, he calmly sat himself back in his booster seat and buckled himself in.

It's true, you know. That statement from a five-year-old boy was an announcement from Heaven. There's more! There's power, and we must learn how to operate in it with wisdom and the supervision of Holy Spirit! There is work to be done and an inheritance to be received and passed on! We have been given the opportunity and the responsibility to carry the fire and fervency of Holy Spirit.

We have this mantle! It's not just a sentimental heirloom; it's power that must be shown! We are His heirs, and we must believe the love that He has for us and allow that love to be shed abroad in our hearts to others. We must allow the gifts of Holy Spirit to work through us and the fruit of the Spirit to be revealed in us. (See 1 Corinthians 12:1-11 and Galatians 5:22-23.) We are His vessels! We are carriers of the mantle. It's not just what we do in a church setting, it's who we are meant to be—glory-carriers releasing power that provokes revival! The power is in us, and it goes with us everywhere we go! We must learn how to use it! The world will not be impacted by mere words alone. Our words must be accompanied and backed up with evidence of Christ's existence.

I am not implying that we don't need "church services." It must be understood that our gatherings are very important. However, I do believe that God is making us aware that even our gatherings must become more intentionally geared toward creating an atmosphere that is conducive for His abiding presence so that we can hear and receive from Him. There must be such a flow of anointing in our gatherings that all will encounter Him and emerge from those times equipped and armed with current revelation from the Lord! If we truly gather on purpose for God's purposes, Holy Spirit will work among us.

He will impart to us relevant wisdom, instruction, and understanding that will enable us to make right decisions, to pray effective prayers, and to rightly discern our times and seasons so that we know what to do.

A ministry friend of mine once said, "God looks into our meetings, and He seeks to find people who are willing to gather and operate in order and alignment with His leading. Over those who are willing to align with Him, God will release His power, and there will be an opening of the heavens that will form. And it won't just be about Heaven coming down to touch earth, but in you, a window will be opened that will cause what's in you to be activated."

One day I was thinking about that statement, and I heard the Lord say:

I Am come to awaken that which is in my people! There are seeds of purpose that I have placed in you that are necessary for this moment, but those seeds have been overshadowed by your emotions. But it's time for the seeds to mature and produce the fruit of My intended purposes! So, I say to you, I will look into your gatherings, and when I find hearts that are aligned with and focused on Me, I will form an opening *over* you through which I will come in the power of My glory and provoke an opening *in* you...My Light will penetrate and remove the shadow that is being cast by your emotions, and My anointing will unlock those seeds of purpose! The unlocking of the seeds will relieve that pressure that has surrounded your mind in this past season, and you will take a deep breath in My presence and feel life and vitality rush into you, empowering you to run with the purpose that is being unlocked!

In this critical hour, God is once again awakening the Church. He is provoking us to take our place and use the power! It's time! Those who have gone before us received this inheritance and invested it wisely for their time. Now, as the recipients of that inheritance, we must do the same.

The mantle *is* weighty, but we must choose to carry it! He assures us that its weight will be absorbed by our passion for Him. The cost *is* great, but we can know for certain that the cause is worth it and the reward is greater! There is no cost too great! The revealed glory of God is worth it all! So, run on, warriors! It's our time to carry the mantle! We must put ourselves in the storyline, and make this our prayer:

Alas, this cross that I must bear, 'tis not a task for me. Its weight is light, for my delight is to do all that You ask of me! I'm turning now to see Your face; 'tis all that matters to me! I lift mine eyes. Lord, hear my cry: SHOW ME YOUR GLORY!

5

Movement in the Hill Country

Now give me this hill country that the LORD promised me that day. You yourself heard then that the Anakites were there and their cities were large and fortified, but, the LORD helping me, I will drive them out just as he said.

Joshua 14:12 NIV

A FEW YEARS AGO, I WAS ASKING THE LORD to reveal to me what He was saying to and about the Church. His response was such a profound insight for me: "Sometimes what I Am saying is what I have already said. If you will recall what I have said, then you will find clarity for what I Am saying now." Many times, when a prophetic word is given, there are those who feel if it doesn't happen right away then it was a false prophesy. We must understand that more often than not, true prophetic words are not just about the moment in which they are given, but God is speaking to us ahead of time concerning a time that is yet to come.

In John 13, Jesus knew that the time was approaching when He would depart from this world, and so He began to speak to

His disciples about some things that would come to pass. Then He said:

> *From now on, I Am telling you [what will happen] before it occurs, so that when it does take place you may believe that I Am He [Who I say I Am—the Christ, the Anointed, the Messiah].*

John 13:19 AMP

When the time comes for a word to be fulfilled, what He spoke ahead of time will validate and give clarity for what He is doing in the current time.

So, this is one of those moments when the Lord is provoking us to revisit some things, He has shown us and spoken to us previously because we are now beginning to see them unfold as they have entered their prophetic timing. As we recall those things (whether dreams, words, decrees, assignments, etc.) and see them from the perspective of where we are now, we can find insight, understanding, and even strategy for what God is saying and doing in this time.

One of the words He has had me revisit recently is a word He spoke to me in May of 2020. The word began with the phrase, "There is movement in the hill country." It was such a different word, and I really had no idea what it meant, but it felt urgent. I presented it to a friend, who also shared it with a leader of a prayer network in the state of Texas, thinking that it might mean something to him since there is a portion of that state that is known as "The Hill Country." Neither of us had any real revelation concerning the word, so I just tucked it aside. Though it felt urgent, I have learned that at the right time, the Lord will always give clarity and understanding for what He speaks to us.

I will share this word in its entirety in just a moment, but first, allow me to share how the Lord brought it back to my remembrance. I feel this will help give some further enlightenment as we look into its current relevance.

At the beginning of this year, I began reading through the Bible, starting in Genesis. As I was reading through the first few books of the Bible, I began to notice that over and over, each time I would read the name, Hebron, it seemed to be being highlighted to me for some reason. I felt the Lord was wanting me to see something in this, but it wasn't until I got to the Book of Joshua that I received the revelation. In the Book of Joshua, Hebron begins to be referred to as "the hill country." As I read that phrase, the word from 2020 immediately was brought back to my mind, and I went to my notes to search it out.

Let me just make a quick interjection here. This is why I often encourage people to write down or record and date any and all words, dreams, visions, scriptures, or revelations they receive from the Lord. The things He reveals may not be for that particular moment, but if it's truly from Him, there will come a time when those things will become necessary. So, we need to steward all things well so that He can instruct us and reveal to us their purpose in their right time.

When the Lord reminded me of the word He spoke to me on May 15, 2020, I was able to retrieve it and begin the journey of allowing Him to unfold its meaning and its message. I found that this word had now become very relevant for where we are and for what we are moving into. Following is the word in its entirety:

> There is movement in the hill country. As the shepherds of old experienced the surrounding of the hosts of Heaven, so again, there is a visitation, a surrounding that will bring forth an earth-shaking announcement. The angels are on the move to announce the coming move of My Spirit. This

announcement will shake the earth. Watch for the movement in the hill country!

Though I didn't fully understand the word when it was first given to me, as I revisited it, I felt the urgency of its significance. For several days, Holy Spirit unveiled some amazing, current revelation to me from that word.

One thing that was shown to me in connection to Hebron, was the remembrance of a word that God gave to Chuck Pierce to release to Dutch Sheets back in early 2017 saying, "It's time to pioneer Hebron again." At that time, God gave Dutch some amazing revelation about Hebron, which, in turn, gave necessary insight and understanding of some things that we were moving into as a nation and as the Body of Christ. Dutch's message entitled *Pioneering Hebron* can still be found online, and I highly recommend that you search it out and listen to its content which is still very relevant and revelatory for us today.

Just a few days after God began to remind me of this word, I attended a meeting in Middletown, Ohio at Oasis Church with my friends, Tim and Carol Sheets. In that meeting, both Tim Sheets and Chuck Pierce shared visions they each had been given from the Lord, in which they saw warring angels *surrounding* the perimeter of the United States and all fifty state capitals. Neither Tim nor Chuck knew what the other was going to be speaking about that night. But, as they spoke, I knew the Lord was giving me further confirmation of the now current relevance of that word from 2020.

As I sat in that meeting at Oasis Church, hearing the confirmation and recalling again the content of what the Lord had spoken to me those years prior, I heard Him say, "The time for this word has come!" I cannot describe the excitement I felt as I realized that the movement of the angelic hosts would now lead us to the announcement of the next "earth-shaking" move of God.

About a week following that meeting, the revival outpouring began at Asbury University. I was so happy to hear about the hunger for Jesus that was being ignited in the hearts of those college students, but there was a weightiness in the Spirit that let us know that there was more to this than a momentary stirring!

As I continued to pray about all of this unfolding revelation, Holy Spirit began to show me another connection with the word from 2020. He reminded me of three dreams that I had received between 2020 and 2022. One was the "Mantle of Revival" dream, that I previously discussed in chapter three of this book. The other dreams were those in which God revealed that He would be reopening some old revival wells. In those dreams, He also made us aware of a coming culmination of the past moves of His Spirit and releasing of the arrows of His purposes that will ignite revival fire all across this nation and spearhead an even greater move in our time. You can find those two dreams, in their entirety, recorded in my book, *Dreams of Awakening*.

I didn't tell anyone that those dreams were once again being highlighted to me. I just began to pray into them and seek the Lord for instruction concerning His purpose for having me revisit them. I found it shocking and quite amazing that almost instantly, people just randomly began to send me video links, posts, and articles in which I or others had previously mentioned those dreams.

Then, out of the blue, my friend Larry Sparks sent me a link for an interview that he and I had recorded in August of 2021, in which we discussed in great detail two of those dreams. The interview had never been aired. Then suddenly, eighteen months after its recording, the video was released for the first time. What

I had perceived as a delay, God knew it was about right timing. Imagine that!

So, God was definitely speaking again through those dreams, and I knew He was somehow connecting them to the word from 2020. But what was the connection? Each of those dreams specifically highlighted past moves of God that had taken place in the mountains of North Carolina and Tennessee and in Southeastern Kentucky. Then it dawned on me that all of these places are often referred to as the hill country. The hills of Kentucky, the hills of Tennessee, and the hills of North Carolina.

And now, it was happening again! There was a fresh outpouring happening at Asbury University in the hills of Kentucky, and it had spread to Lee University in the hills of Tennessee! The announcement was resounding that the next move of God was being reignited, and it was beginning in the "Hill Country"! The wells were being reopened and beginning to burst forth again! The angels were on the move, and the earth-shaking announcement was now being declared! This is what God had told us to "watch for"! There is movement in the hill country!

As exciting as this is, we must understand that the initial outpouring is just the beginning! It was just the announcement, letting us know that greater things are yet to come. It was the signal that had set other things into motion for the coming, greater move of God's Spirit in the earth!

This very thing was demonstrated in the dream I was given about the reopening of the revival well at the Red River Meeting House in Kentucky. In that dream, the well erupted like a geyser, but as amazing as that was, the eruption was not a spectacle to just stand in awe of; it was a sign that was accompanied by a signal that provoked continued movement. The announcement came, "It's time," and the eagles were dispatched to carry and release the arrows and waters of revival. The rapid response teams were sent out with assignments that had to do with spearheading another greater move of God in our time!

We have witnessed the beginning of the movement, but we can't just stop and marvel as though that's all there is! I believe Jesus is now saying to His Body, "Yes, the movement is happening. The wells are opened! Pay attention to the signal and move into your place without hesitation." The movement in the hill country should provoke movement in us! God has given undeniable confirmation in all of this that it's time for us to advance and possess the fullness of His promises that have now intersected their prophetic timing! We must align with Christ and move with Him!

Pioneer Hebron Again

Remember the thing that God used to bring about the resurgence of the word that was given in 2020—and had now come into its time in 2023—was Holy Spirit's highlighting the name Hebron as I was reading through the Bible. Hebron is a very significant place, and when we understand its significance, we gain even more insight into what God is revealing to us now.

It was at Hebron that God came to Abraham for the final time and said, "You are going to have a son next year." So, Hebron is a place that represents the fulfillment of seemingly impossible promises!

Hebron is the place where David was anointed to rule Israel. So, Hebron represents a place of anointing and positioning.

Hebron is also the "hill country" that was promised to Caleb when they entered Canaan. Others said, "It can't be done." Caleb said, "Give me my mountain!" The timing of God pushed Caleb forward with a confident knowing that he was well able to possess the promise! So, Hebron represents the place where timing and destiny meet together to provoke pioneers to press past fear and take out the giants that are occupying their promises!

The reason God is connecting that word from 2020 to Hebron is that this is part of the movement that has been set into motion. It's time for some seemingly impossible promises to be fulfilled. It's a time when God is going to position us to fulfill the purposes for which He has anointed us! Destiny and timing have met, and we must decide whether or not we're going to advance with God and occupy that which He has said belongs to us! The announcement has been declared, and the movement has started. It's time for the Church to rise up and pioneer Hebron again. It's time to rise up with confidence in our great God, Whose hand is good upon us, and drive out the giants to reclaim our rightful inheritance.

This is the transition point. The move is on! Awakening has begun. This is it! We must listen, and follow God as He leads us forward to accomplish all that He has determined for us to do in this moment. It's time for an earth-shaking movement of the Spirit of God, and there must be rapid response on the part of the Ekklesia! We cannot be afraid to move with Him! We all have a part in the plan of God for this time, and whatever He leads us to do, we must advance quickly with a confident knowing that we have been anointed to do it!

It's time for some bold, courageous, and uncompromised faith in God to arise in us that provokes us to believe Him and work with Holy Spirit to do our part! He's calling us to position!

Father, we see that the movement of which You prophesied in 2020 has now begun. We have stepped into a transitional time.

The angels are on the move, announcing the unfolding of the next great move of Your Spirit. It's happening, and we want to move with You! Thank You for speaking to us ahead of time in order to give clarity and validation for what is happening now in this time.

Thank You for what You have done at Asbury University and for the sparks of revival that were ignited on other college campuses, churches, schools, and towns across America and in different parts of the world. The movement has started, but this is only just the beginning. We set our faces toward You. We will listen for Your instructions, and we will rise in obedience to You as Holy Spirit leads us into the fulfillment of Your promises that have now intersected their prophetic timing. We will step where You order, as You position us to fulfill every purpose for which You have anointed us! We will work with You to possess all that You have given! We will not give in to fear that causes hesitation, but we will move quickly at Your command! We will advance into this movement with boldness, courage, and uncompromised faith to move forward and to do our part for our times! In Jesus' Name! Amen!

6

Take Your Seat

For this cause everyone who is godly shall pray to You in a time when You may be found; surely in a flood of great waters they shall not come near him. You are my hiding place; You shall preserve me from trouble; You shall surround me with songs of deliverance. Selah. I will instruct you and teach you in the way you should go; I will guide you with My eye.

Psalm 32:6-8 NKJV

ONE DAY AS I WAS DRIVING DOWN THE INTERSTATE, I heard the Lord say to me, "Buckle your seatbelt! Here we go!" I instantly got that feeling that you get when you are sitting in the seat of an airplane. You're buckled in, awaiting the inevitable takeoff. You feel the momentum increase as you leave the gentle taxiing down the runway. Suddenly, the engines roar, and the adrenaline kicks in as you gain speed. The thrust then leads to lift-off, and everything that you planned and prepared for, talked about, learned about, and anticipated just got very real! The remembrance of all the steps and preparation that led to this moment provokes a confident assurance that whatever is ahead, you are ready. There's nothing but forward!

Yeah, this feels just like that kind of moment! We are being transitioned and positioned to fulfill the purposes for which we have been anointed. This moment is what we've been prepared for! It's here! It's happening, and now it's time to take our seat in Christ, obey our Guide, and trust God as He launches us into the next earth-shaking movement of His Spirit!

Many have relegated the movement and power of God to just what happens within our church buildings. To some, the movement of God is just a momentary provocation of deep and intense emotional feelings that come and go. To others, the power of God is only relegated to the manifestations of supernatural miracles, signs, and wonders. These functions *are* absolutely the evidence and results of the demonstrated movement and power of God. However, we must never attempt to put Him in a box and believe that's all there is! As great as these things are, there is still so much more for us to experience in Him! We must never put limits on what we believe God can do in and through those who have faith in Him. As great as you can imagine Him to be, He is greater still! Our minds can never grasp the vastness of His power. To try to do so is to limit our ability to see and experience Him in His fullness! As someone once said, "Isn't it great to serve a God Who can never be exaggerated?"

Our corporate church gatherings are very important, and the Lord will certainly come in the awesomeness of His presence when we assemble ourselves in united worship to Him. I have experienced amazing and life-marking encounters with Him in many church gatherings. As I have discussed in depth in previous chapters of this book, we see without doubt that the manifestations of power and of the Spirit, as He works through us and among us with miracles, signs, and wonders are also definite and determined ways that God desires to make Himself known! Still, it must be understood that, as amazing and necessary as all of these expressions of God are, these are not the only ways He reveals His power and movement. He also works through us in very practical ways as we purposefully submit our lives to Him as willing vessels.

There is a place for each one of us, and every part matters. Paul instructed Timothy to stay steady and to fully carry out his ministry (see 2 Timothy 4:5). Ministry is not just about that which is done from a sanctuary platform. The word *ministry* translates to mean "attendance (as a servant); or service" (Strong's Exhaustive Concordance, G1248). Ministry is availing ourselves to the Lord so that He can work through us however He chooses to reveal Himself to the world around us.

Platform ministry is a part of Kingdom work, but it's not the only part. Some will work in the Church. Some will work in the marketplace. Some will work in governmental positions. Some will work in educational positions. Some will work in prayer closets. Some will work in their families. Some will work in the medical field. Some will work as business owners, authors, or seamstresses. Some will work as carpenters, plumbers, or brick masons. Some will work as missionaries and volunteers. Some will work as ministers, teachers, pastors, evangelists, prophets, and apostles. Some will work with the youth. Some will visit hospitals and nursing homes. Some will work in prayer assignments.

We all have a part, and the bottom line is this: Whatever He tells you to do, do it—whatever, whenever, wherever, and however He tells you to do it, do it with all of your might! Listen to His voice, obey His commands. Let us all do our part!

We must become more aware of His Spirit and familiar with His voice. As we go about our daily lives, we must remain alert and available to Him at all times. His instructions and leading may not always come by way of an audible voice. Sometimes there will be just a subtle feeling that we get from Him.

Sometimes it will be a knowing deep in our spirit that we should do a certain thing or go to a certain place. It may be a word we hear in a sermon or something we read in a book that will spark an idea in us. However Holy Spirit chooses to lead and instruct us, we must be available and listening, and we must be willing and obedient to follow through. Instant and complete obedience, even in the most unsuspecting and seemingly insignificant tasks, will often provoke the most powerful outcomes.

Our spiritual inheritance is rich in all things good! *"Every good gift and every perfect gift is from above"* (James 1:17 KJV). God has given us Holy Spirit, Who makes known and imparts to us these good things. By His presence and supervision in our lives, God empowers us to know and do things that we couldn't possibly know or do within our own ability and understanding. He reveals to us ideas, concepts, and insights. He teaches us the principles of the Kingdom. He helps us to make right decisions in every situation. Christ dwells in us by the Spirit, and He gives us unlimited access to power, strength, and wisdom to walk the path God has ordained for our lives. He enables us to fully achieve all of the purposes He has for us. Holy Spirit is our Helper. He is our Guide. As we learn to walk in cooperation with Him, to become familiar with His leading, and to recognize that inward witness, He will order our steps. As we step where He orders, He causes us to flourish in the things we have been anointed to do, and this, in itself, becomes a testimony to the world around us. As they see us accomplishing and thriving in ways that are beyond our human ability, they are left with no explanation other than "it had to be God."

Moses asked the Lord to show him His glory, and God's response to that was, *"I will let My goodness be seen"* (Exodus 33:19 paraphrased). There are people in the world who do not know

God. They don't know Jesus as Savior and Lord. We who do know Him are His witnesses. What He does in our lives becomes a revelation of His reality, a light that shines to those in darkness. Many people will never come to our church gatherings, but we, His witnesses, are with them daily in the marketplace, in our workplaces, in school, and in our homes. As they see our lives being impacted by God in these practical demonstrations that are the result of His influence upon us, these demonstrations then become effective ways in which He manifests His goodness, power, and Person to them. The goodness of God being revealed through our lives—even in the most practical ways—can be just as powerful and life-changing as when He flows through us with miracles, signs, and wonders. The power is in the glory—the revealed reality of God.

Awakening the Laborers

As the message of a third Great Awakening circulates through our sermons and social media posts, we must understand that the awakening must begin among the people of God. The Church is filled with laborers, who are anointed to reap and tend to the harvest, but many are still asleep. Without the laborers, there can be no harvest. So, God is waking up the laborers. Paul said, *"And that, knowing the time, that now it is high time to awake out of sleep"* (Romans 13:11 KJV).

The born-again experience is not just to get us to Heaven, and it's not just some membership to the "church social club." It is the gateway to a relationship with God. Jesus is the Door! He gives us access to all that God is and has. It's time for the harvesters to rise up and be endued with the power that has been made available to us—and go and BE! Be who God created us to be. Do what He calls us to do! Utilize the fullness of all that we have been given. Take up the cross and follow Him!

In my first book, *Awakening the Church to Awaken a Nation*, I shared a vision the Lord once gave to me. I feel this vision will give us more clarity for what I am writing about in this chapter.

> A few years ago, God showed to me a vision in which I saw an army of people, who were lying on the ground all over a field. They were dressed in what I would describe as biblical army attire. They appeared to be dead, but in my spirit, I knew they were not dead. What I heard was, "They are exhausted." Then all of a sudden, a sound was released, and immediately, upon the release of this sound, every soldier was renewed with strength, and they simultaneously stood to their feet, got positioned, and were ready to move. And then I heard loudly and adamantly, "Wake up the warriors!"

I was going to be speaking at a conference a couple of days after that, so I thought maybe the purpose of the vision was that the Lord was giving me a sermon title and a prophetic directive for the upcoming meeting. After about an hour of study, I still had no direction for the message that I thought I was being led to preach, so I asked the Lord what this vision was about. He then said to me so clearly, "I Am not giving you a *sermon*; I Am giving you a *mandate*. Wake up My warriors!"

For countless people in the Body of Christ, this has been one of the most difficult seasons we have ever faced. I hear it almost everywhere I go, and it's not just one thing happening, but there are many things coming from seemingly every direction—spiritually, emotionally, financially, and physically. The result of the pressure of this last season has left many feeling completely exhausted, but the Wind is blowing! Take a breath! Breathe in hope! Perk up your spiritual ears and listen for the sound! God is awakening His Church. We've been lulled to sleep by pressures and distractions. We have worn ourselves out with struggles (some necessary, some not so much), but we have entered a whole new era, and everything is changing.

This is an urgent moment, and we don't have time to hesitate! God is calling! I see Him walking through America, calling, *"My Church, My Church, where are you? Come out of hiding, shake off the debris of compromise, fear, and pride! Awaken! Be clothed with My glory! I Am calling you!"*

At a gathering in 2016, the Lord spoke through me the following urgent and passionate word:

> To My Church I say, awake, awake! Be clothed in My strength. Take your place. Arise! Hear My sound echoing through this time, declaring awakening to the Body of Christ. Though you were dead, yet you shall live, and through you I will now begin to reveal My manifested glory. As you arise, I will arise, and every enemy will scatter! Watch and see and be amazed by what I will do in days ahead through My awakened Body.

It's time for us to awaken out of our slumber and complacency. We can no longer see ministry as just being that which a few select people do from a pulpit or in a church setting. The Lord has need of all of us, and He is calling the harvesters to awaken and to position ourselves to work with Him.

I remember that, when I was a young girl, my mom would call to me in the mornings to wake up and get ready for school. Not wanting to leave the comfort of my warm bed and arouse from my sleep, I would linger. A few minutes would pass, and she would call again. Finally, she would turn on the light, call me by my full name, and demand that I get up. By this time, her call was no longer, "Wake up!" The time had become urgent. The bus would be arriving soon, so now, her call was, "Get up and get ready to go!"

The warriors have been awakened, but awakening is no longer enough! Now, we must rise up and be ready to advance! The light is on! The time is urgent! The Lord of the harvest is calling the laborers to position ourselves to move with Him! Delay is not an option! We each have a part, a place, and we must follow His guidance, receive His power, and allow Him to work through us to accomplish the purposes for which He sends us! We must learn to use what He has given to us and work with Him to see His will being done "on earth as it is in Heaven." Even our practical deeds can be profound expressions of His power and presence to those around us. We must submit to Holy Spirit so that through a kind word or gesture, or even a smile, we can release life-changing power to those around us. In all our ways, as we walk and work with the Lord, He can reach through us to accomplish His will and make Himself known.

Last year, I had a profound dream that illustrates all of this so vividly.

I dreamed there was a man walking along a beach. I first saw the feet of this man. He had on black leather, laced-up combat boots. He wore a long, button-up shirt with no collar—the length of it going to just above his knees—and khaki pants that were rolled up to just below his knees.

I then saw a flowery archway and white chairs that were set up for a wedding. There were two sections of chairs with an aisle between them. It wasn't yet time for the wedding, so the guests were gathered under a pavilion on the other side of the sand dune. The man walking on the beach was the groom. He was walking up and down the beach, diligently searching for the bride.

Unable to find her, he looked up to see his dad standing on top of the dune. His dad, knowing he hadn't found the bride yet, said, "Whistle for her!"

So, the groom walked further down the beach and went around a bend, and he began to whistle a song that I recognized as a song that we often sing to the Lord, but in the dream, the groom was whistling it to the bride. The words to that portion of the song are "My beloved is the most beautiful among thousands and thousands." He did not sing this song; he only whistled the tune.

Across the dune, he then faintly heard the voice of his bride. I knew that this was a song that he had often sung to her, so when he whistled the tune, she recognized it and cried out, "I'm here! I'm here!"

He climbed to the top of the dune and could see, way out from there, a forest. Between him and the forest, there was a wide swath of land that looked like a savannah. I could see that on that savannah was a wolf pack. There were six wolves, and they were trotting along, single file, in an "S" pattern. I knew these wolves were chasing the bride. She had been running from them through that forest and across that savannah, and now she was hiding in fear at the base of the dune in some tall grass and brambles. I knew the wolves felt that she had nowhere to go because she had no way to get up the tall dune.

The groom saw her hiding in the grass, and he said, "Come to me."

She said, "I'm afraid, and I can't get up there."

He pointed to his left and said, "Here's a path."

It was as if that path had just formed, and so she ran up the path to him. She was wearing her wedding dress, but she was very disheveled. Her hair was all messed up, and she had a rip in the lower right front portion of her dress. She lifted her dress just enough for him to see that her feet were bleeding because she had been running barefoot through that forest and across that savannah.

He then said, "No wonder you are afraid. You didn't wear the shoes I gave you."

She said, "I have them." She had been carrying the shoes, but she didn't put them on. That's when I saw that her shoes were boots, just like the ones he was wearing.

He said, "Carrying them won't help you. You have to wear them. I gave them to you so you could wear them." And then He said, "Come with me."

He offered her his arm, and she put her hand in the bend of his elbow and walked with him. He led her back down the beach to a rock formation that was situated next to the water. This was a very large and tall rock, and it was flat on the top. He knew the way to ascend, and He led her to the top of the rock. There were two chairs there, and he motioned for her to sit down in one of them. He then bent down on one knee and helped her get her boots on. He laced up the boots, and while he was bent down, helping with the boots, he also sewed up the rip in her dress.

It still wasn't quite time for the wedding, and so they sat together in those chairs so they could be alone and so she could rest. As they sat there, the wind began to blow, and it blew her hair back into place. It became beautifully styled.

They were facing the ocean. From time to time, there would be very large waves that would form and come toward them, and she would start to get afraid.

He would say, "You don't have to be afraid. You have your shoes on."

She said, "But my shoes won't help me with that."

He said, "Watch *me*." He said this in a way that made her look at him. With her eyes then focused on him, she was able to watch his responses to the waves. And as she would watch his reactions, he was actually teaching her what to do.

When the waves would form, he would just start laughing. Sometimes he would laugh so hard, he would slap his leg. As he did this, the waves would settle down before they ever reached the rock. This happened several times, so she began to do as he did. When the waves would form, she would laugh and laugh with him, and the waves would settle down.

Then, after a while, all of a sudden, a massive tsunami wave formed very near to the shore. This time he did not laugh. His entire expression changed. He wasn't afraid. He looked angry. The bride started to get afraid because something was different about this wave.

The groom looked around her to his right, and he saw that the guests were now gathering for the wedding and being seated in the white chairs on the beach. He knew this wave would kill all of those people if it came ashore.

He said to the bride, "This time we have to stand!"

So, they stood up, and she put her hand in the bend of his elbow again.

Then he looked out at that wave and shook his head, and he spoke to it in a stern, loud voice, adamantly saying, "IT IS *NOT* TIME!"

The bride then joined her voice with his, and together they said those words to the massive wave over and over, "IT IS *NOT* TIME!"

The wave kept getting bigger and bigger, as if taunting them, but they continued to stand and declare, "NO! IT IS *NOT* TIME!"

The wave then got right up to where they were standing, and it crashed at the base of the rock. The water even came up onto the rock, but the groom held on to the bride. They were not moved by the wave, and even their chairs were not moved. The wave settled down and did not go past the rock. It never made it to where the people were sitting.

He then looked at the bride and said, "Are you ready for the wedding?"

And she said, "I am now!" And they walked together toward the chairs and the floral archway.

That was the end of the dream.

This dream is not so much about Eschatology, as it is about our covenantal relationship with the Lord. It's about understanding our role as the Church here in the earth. Jesus is calling His Bride to come out of hiding! We must wake up to the revelation that we have been running from—and fearful of—the very things that He has given us authority to conquer. We have been allowing ourselves to live in a state of spiritual poverty because we have failed to "put on" the shoes of the gospel of peace, which He has given to us!

He is saying to us,

It's time for you to see the path I have laid before you. My strong right arm is extended to you. Take it and follow Me into the place of revelation and understanding of the position I have made available to you!

There are some evil risings that are threatening certain destruction and hostile takeover of our lives, our children, our nation, and even our churches, but Paul said that the Lord has made us to sit together with Him in the heavenly places (see Ephesians 2:6). It's a picture of the position of authority and power that we are called to exemplify as the Bride of Christ, and it's time for us to take our seat and work with Him!

You may have thought, "I don't feel like a warrior!" I said that to the Lord one time, and He said to me, "*You may not have always felt like a warrior, but I have always seen the warrior in you!*" Warriors are not super-human! We are simply human, but, in our humanity, Jesus has given us access to an inheritance that enables us to do the works that He has done and "even greater"! It's not about our human abilities. What Jesus is looking for is faith—faith in God! Faith that comes from the revelation of the greatness of Who our God is! Faith that keeps us focused on Him, regardless of the waves that may threaten to overtake us! We don't see the waves; we see our righteous King Jesus, and we imitate Him! We stand without wavering! We persevere and refuse to retreat! We wear our armor! We pull necessary tools from our inheritance, and we take ground! We trust and acknowledge Him in all our ways, and He reveals through us His might, wisdom, and authority! These are the attributes of a true warrior. It's not by our might or strength; it is by His Spirit in us that we are made to sit with Him! *He makes us brave!*

So, take your seat! You have a place in the plan of God! It's time to wear your shoes, be clothed in your spiritual armor, and allow the Wind of the Spirit to revive and restore you so that you can rule and reign with Christ as His joint-heir! He's calling for you! Hear His whistle. You are His beloved, and He has need of you! Respond to His song. Come out of hiding! See and take the path that He is revealing to you in this time! Rise up, warrior, and focus on the One Who calls you His own! Watch Him! He will guide you with His eye!

We must rely on His strength and walk with Him, stay close enough to watch Him and be willing to imitate Him. As we do these things, we will see His purposes accomplished and His will being done. Then when the time does come, we will be ready for the wedding!

Father, our minds can never grasp the vastness of Your power! Your ways and thoughts are so much higher than ours. On our own, we could never achieve the fulfillment of Your desire for us to be Your witnesses in all of the earth. But You have given us Your Holy Spirit, Who imparts to us the fullness of all that You are, and He enables us, in our human flesh, to walk in Your supernatural power and to make You known. Even in the most practical ways, we can release the Light of Christ so that those in darkness can be drawn to Him and made free.

Teach me, Lord, to walk in full cooperation with Holy Spirit, to become more familiar with His leading and to recognize that inward witness, as He orders my steps. Help me to put on my shoes of peace, and without hesitation to step where He orders.

May those within Your Ekklesia take our seat, Lord, and watch and imitate You. May we all humble ourselves to work with You to accomplish Your purposes. It is not by our might or power but by Your Spirit that we can be effective in the things that You have anointed and called us to do. We declare that Your beloved is coming out of hiding! We are rising as Your heirs, and through us, You will shine the light of Your glory to bring a great awakening to our nation and to our world! In Jesus' Name, we pray! Amen!

7

A Big Picture Moment

Yet who knows whether you have come to the Kingdom [been positioned] for such a time as this?

Esther 4:14 NKJV (paraphrase mine)

THE PAST FEW MONTHS SEEM TO HAVE USHERED many into a deepening passion for the awakening, which has begun to broaden in scope and increased momentum. There's an unshakeable feeling that we have crossed into the unfolding of a history-making moment. As a matter of fact, the Lord recently said to me that this moment will be "one for the history books."

The Lord is calling every member of His Body to rise and shine with the Light of His glory. We must be alert and obedient to His voice. There are things we have seen and done in past seasons that were necessary, and even powerful, but I just have a feeling that Holy Spirit is saying, "You ain't seen nothing yet!" We have come to a "for such a time as this" type moment, and the Lord has need of His Ekklesia. As His governing body, we should be legislating and implementing His Kingdom purposes, not just reacting to hell's attempts to change times and laws and to overthrow our Christian heritage. The Ekklesia should be raising the standard, presenting Christ, and working with Him to advance His righteous cause that has the power to affect the whole of society, as the reality of His transforming glory is released through our obedience to Him. It's time, and He is provoking us to position ourselves to work with Him in this hour.

The Pieces are Coming Together

One Sunday afternoon, I was having lunch with some friends. During our conversation, I shared with them a revelation that the Lord once gave to me about "marked moments." Through that revelation, He helped me to understand that there are some things He leads us to do that, at that particular time, may seem to make no sense to our human understanding, but He assured me that all the pieces are necessary. He said, "Those times of obedience are pieces of a bigger picture. In and of themselves, they may seem to be irrelevant and even senseless, but there will come a time when I will put all the pieces together, and you will understand why each part was necessary."

We are each on a journey with the Lord, and as we follow Him in faith and obedience, He leads us according to His plan. Even when we don't understand the steps, we must stay the course so that, in the right time, the parts can be placed to form the whole of God's intentions.

As I shared this revelation with my friends that day, I heard myself say, "This is the time when the pieces are coming together." Instantly, we all knew that Holy Spirit had come to the table and entered our conversation. We all felt His presence, and the weight of those words was undeniable. "The pieces are coming together." That means that we have moved into a "big picture" moment. Something has been completed, and now the purpose for those "marked moments" will begin to be revealed, and we will be so thankful that we took the journey!

The big picture not only validates our faith walk in times past, it also unveils understanding that lends itself to prophetic insight for where we are going. Moses stood before twelve men that he had sent to scope out the land to determine Israel's next move. Ten of them said, "We can't take that land. The giants are huge, and we are like grasshoppers compared to them." But Joshua and Caleb had gotten a revelation of the big picture. Their report went something like this: "This is what it's all been about. Everything God has done has led us to this moment. His hand is good upon us, and we are well able to possess what He has promised." (See Numbers 13:30.) The pieces had come together, and the "big picture" had made them acutely aware that it was now time to cross over and take the land.

Their arrival in the land did not mean that their journey was done or that everything would be easy from that point forward. The journey would continue, and there were still battles to be fought, but the journey had shifted from circling the familiar path around the mountain to moving into the land that God said they could and would possess.

God is saying to us, "The pieces are coming together." A shift is happening, and we are feeling the provocation of the Lord to focus forward with new perspective. It's not a time to settle or wrongly assess the future and our ability to step into it victoriously. It's not time to go back and do what has already been done. It's time to be bold and courageous and possess the land! Consider the following vision that the Lord recently gave to me:

> I saw a vision of a deep and wide chasm. On the other side of the chasm, I could see a well-formed pathway that was glowing. I knew the glow was actually the glory of God that was covering the path. The only way to get to the pathway was to cross the ravine, and the

only way across it was a tightrope. I could see a line of people, who would walk up to the edge, and while they desired to go to the other side, fear of the chasm overpowered their desire for the glory, and they turned and walked away. Then there was a voice that thundered, saying, *"Trust the Lord and fear not!"*

I saw another group of people who then came to the edge. They saw the chasm, but their desire for the glory overpowered their fear of the chasm, and they courageously began to take steps on the tightrope. As they did, angels began surrounding them, assisting them to cross over.

I then heard the Lord say, *"You are now at a critical point. Your past obedience has led you to this moment and has created supply for your future, but you must choose to go over the chasm. I have provided a way, but it is a way that requires you to completely trust in Me. Your first steps will take a courageous act of faith in Me, but as you move, you will find that I have provided divine assistance. I have commanded the hosts to assist you, and they hearken unto My voice. I have placed My Spirit within you, and as you hearken to His voice and leading, the narrow way won't seem so daunting. For those who choose to trust Me and fear not, you will find strength and ability to traverse the tight places and enter the way that is filled with My manifested glory."*

I believe the Lord is saying to the remnant that will boldly proceed with trust in Him, "The culmination of all that you have heard, seen, believed, and done is about to become the catapult that will launch you into greater encounter, power, and effectiveness!"

This is not a time to hesitate in our response to the Lord. He is giving us this opportunity to see that there is more to come! The path with the glory on it is shining brightly in the distance, and He is beckoning us all to come and walk that path! It's not a proverbial carrot that is being extended, as if it's some type of mirage that we chase after only to find that it won't really be there when we finally get to it. The path represents the unfolding of God's plan. It's time for the next part to be accessed, and He is calling us to position ourselves in such a way that regardless of how things may appear around us, His voice and that path are more real to us than anything else. So real, in fact, that we will be willing to take every necessary step in complete faith and trust in Him in order to reach the goal!

A leap of faith is required in this moment! I have said it so many times, but it must be said again: real faith takes real courage. This is a "real faith and real courage" type moment! Real faith comes from a right focus on God! He doesn't require us to make things happen on our own. All through this book, we have discussed the fact that we have an inheritance that is available for all who have accepted Jesus as Lord of their lives. That inheritance grants us access into the fullness of God. All that He is, has, and can do is imparted to us through the work of Holy Spirit. The inheritance is there, and for those who choose to yield to Holy Spirit, the benefits of that inheritance can and will be gained.

As we focus on God and not on ourselves, faith in Him arises within us. That faith gives us courage to advance. For those who will be willing to trust Him without measure, glory awaits.

We are in a time when God is transitioning and positioning the Ekklesia for what is ahead. The Wind of the Spirit is blowing again, and He is breathing resurrection life into the Body. The laborers are being positioned with authority and boldness for the reaping of the harvest that is ripe. I once heard Pastor Kent Christmas make this true and relevant statement: "You can't reap a harvest without laborers. This move we have entered into will not be about preachers, but it will be about the Body of Christ, anointed with the power of the Holy Ghost. What God is doing now is…He's resurrecting the laborers."

God has filled us with His purposes, and we must take those steps of faith so that we can bring forth the fruit of the seeds that He has planted within us!

Hear Him saying:

I Am awakening a word within you. There is a seed, a word, that was planted in you years ago. At the time of its planting, the season was not yet for its revealing. Though you have forgotten, I have continued to watch over that seed. Now, it is time for the fruit to come forth, so I Am awakening the seed, and I will hasten its maturity. I will perform through you the purpose for which I planted it in you! Move in complete obedience to My Spirit as He works the ground [in you] to bring it forth! Work with Him, and its fruit will spring forth speedily!

We have stepped through a major door, and the Lord is calling us to attention for forward advancement. As in the vision about the chasm, some are finding themselves hesitant in their response to His calling and leading. This hesitation could be for many different reasons. Some have fear of the chasm. Others have been wounded in the past, and they are allowing grief and trauma to capture their soul. Others have grown weary in well-doing because they haven't seen that for which they believed, and the promises to which they held seem to have been delayed or misunderstood. They have become shrouded in hope that has been deferred. There are multitudes of excuses—some even seemingly justifiable—that some will use in this critical time. This is why we need a shift in focus. We have to love the Lord more than we fear the chasm. We must yearn to be clothed in His glory more than we want the shroud of past experiences. He must become our greatest desire! We cannot drag our feet in this moment. We cannot allow the difficulties of the past season to cause us to hesitate in our response to the Lord in this season. We cannot allow the uncertainties of the days ahead to provoke fear in us and cause us to miss this big picture moment. We must trust God! Fear not and move forward! The time is now, and the time is urgent!

Harvest the Harvesters

In a dream I once had, someone tossed me a set of keys and said, "You're up, Gina! This is your deal." I felt such a lack of confidence fill my mind, trying to override my faith in God. But there were others who recognized my hesitation and lack of confidence, and they said immediately, "You can do this! You have already been prepared!"

There are times when God will direct us to do things, and our flesh will immediately try to override our faith. Thoughts of our limitations provoke a lack of confidence, even though we know God is speaking! In that moment, we must do as Paul instructed. We must cast down arguments and every high thing that seeks to exalt itself against the knowledge of God, and bring every thought captive to the obedience of Christ (see 2 Corinthians 10:5). Just because thoughts, and even feelings of

97

doubt, fear, insecurity, or intimidation may come, that doesn't mean we just have to accept them as truth! Cast them down by bringing them under subjection to the knowledge of the real truth that is in Christ! What He says about us is truth, and regardless of how we feel or think, if God leads us to do something, we can be assured that He has equipped us to do it! Fear and hesitation are not an option. As those who are truly devoted to Him, trust and obedience are our only options.

I recently had a dream in which we were told that it is time to "harvest the harvesters." I had never heard that phrase before, and I was deeply impacted by its implication! Your part may seem small and insignificant, but it's not! Every part matters! As we each do our part, more and more parts are then awakened. The more parts that are awakened, the more our capacity increases. It's the power of *multiplication*. Through the years, we've been content with only *additions* being made to the Church and, sadly, even sometimes with *subtractions*! But we are in the time when God is declaring multiplication. It reminds me of the words of Jesus when He said, "Pray that the Lord of the harvest will send forth laborers." For far too long there has been way too much complacency in the Church. It's time to get the laborers back to work! This is not the time for us to slack up or hesitate; it's time for us all to do our part.

The Lord once spoke this powerful word to me:

It is time to stand UP, not stand down! Take up the weapons of your warfare—My Word, My Spirit, My characteristics, and the authority of My Name and the power of My blood—and STAND! Stand in prayer! Stand in faith! In the areas where you have been "standing down," you have become vulnerable! It's time to reinforce the ranks. I Am awakening My Body!

So, I say to you, stand up, shake yourself, and hold fast to the liberty I have given to you. Sin shall have no dominion over you. Fear shall have no dominion over you. Grief shall have no dominion over you. Anger shall have no dominion over you. Lack shall have no dominion over you. Curses shall have no dominion over you. NOTHING shall have dominion over you…unless you allow it to have dominion over you! DO NOT allow it! I defeated it all on the cross! Stand under the protection of My blood and the authority of my FINISHED work on the cross!

Many have given other things dominion over their minds and over their bodies; therefore, many have grown weak, thus weakening My BODY! But I Am reinforcing the ranks! I Am releasing My sound this day, and those who hear will shake off the sins and weights that have held them down, and they will stand up! They will rise with repentant hearts, minds that will be changed, eyes that will see, and ears that will hear! My Church, My Body, will rise without spot, wrinkle, or blemish. My Body will rise with renewed strength— My strength, My power, My Spirit in them! And through this glorious Body, I will work a work that will bring shock and awe to the nations and to the Church! There will be an awakening of an awareness of Who I really am. For those who are looking for Me—those who have humbled themselves before Me—it will be a GREAT awakening! For those who have made flesh and other things their god, it will be a RUDE awakening!

There will be an irresistible, unflinching army that will rise, clothed in My power and Person, and through this

Body, My Body, I *will* make Myself known, and you will see that I Am not Who you thought I was…I Am not weak and passive! I Am *not* lacking in power! I Am not slack concerning My promises! I AM The Lord—holy, omnipotent, full of might and strength—the One Who was, is, and is to come, the Almighty! I Am clothed with might and with the Spirit of wisdom and understanding. I speak and mountains melt in My presence! I declare a thing, and it is! My ways and thoughts are higher than yours! I Am holy…I Am…and I WILL make Myself known!

So, stand up! Put on your armor and SHINE with the light of My unavoidable glory! And at My signal, BE ready to go forward!

This is an urgent moment, perhaps the most urgent moment that we have ever known, and in it, the Lord has need of His Body. There are things that are happening in our nation and in our world that will not change until the Body of Christ rises up with the revelation and activation of our spiritual inheritance. We must submit ourselves completely to Him so that the full power of that inheritance can be fully appropriated in and through our lives. It's time to refocus. It's time to reposition. It's time to advance! The prophetic destiny of our nation is at stake. Like Esther of old, we have been brought to this moment to be positioned for the sake of change to provoke a national, and even a worldwide, revival!

To some, America may seem too far gone. The advancement of evil agendas may seem to have prevailed against the prophetic destiny of God for our nation. But through past dreams and prophetic words, we know that God has declared that He is NOT late, and that America *shall* be saved! As I shared earlier, I once had a dream in which I saw eagles carrying and

100

releasing the waters of revival wells that had been reopened. This was signifying that what God has started, even in generations that have gone before us, He intends to continue in even greater measure!

There was a man that stood beside me in that dream, and as we watched the eagles releasing those arrows, we saw America being ignited with the fires of revival. The man then said to me, "This is how America will be saved! Do NOT doubt it! There is coming a sweeping move of the Spirit of God that will ignite the land with the fire of His presence, and *that* will bring a swift and undeniable awakening to an awareness of God."

The timing of God changes everything. We have moved into a moment that has been marked on God's timetable, and it is prompting movement in the Body of Christ. Jesus is stirring His Body to awaken. He is calling us to get up above the noise and chaos surrounding us, to rise above our emotions, and to position ourselves before Him so we can see from His perspective and hear with unhindered clarity what He is saying to us in this moment. Seeing things from His perspective breaks us free from the strongholds of doubt and fear. Hearing His voice delivers us from the grip of anxiety and uncertainty. His Word is truth, and when we know His truth, His truth makes us free (see John 8:32).

Several years ago, the Lord showed to me a vision.

In this vision, I saw a man, sitting in a straight-back chair. His elbows were on his knees and his head propped up in his hands. I could that see his legs and feet were covered with some type of white dust. The man was weeping, and his tears were dropping onto the dust on his legs and feet. The tears were mingling with the dust, causing it to form into blocks of cement.

The man wanted to stand, but he was completely confined by those cement blocks.

Then suddenly, I saw a hand holding a hammer. The hand began swinging the hammer intently, and the cement was broken into pieces, freeing the man to rise up and walk.

God said that His Word is "like a hammer that breaks the rock in pieces" (Jeremiah 23:29). When we allow ourselves to rise above the fray of life and hear Him, His truth is quick and powerful to break us free from those things that have been confining us to fear and other crippling emotions!

The Lord recently said to me, "The winds are changing. Watch for Me. Listen to My voice and obey Me swiftly and completely." Things are happening quickly, and we must be ready and willing to move with Him at a moment's notice. He will speak, and we must respond. Holy Spirit will guide us, and we must follow Him. He will instruct, and we must obey. To do that, we have to allow God to free us from anything that would cause us to hesitate in our obedience to Him. We must resist any form of pride or fear that may try to rise up in us to cause us to defend and hold onto anything that He identifies as a confinement! His purpose in dealing with these things is because He sees and knows that they have the potential to sabotage our destiny in Him! So, we must believe the love that He has for us and allow Him to remove the confinements and to heal us for the purpose of personal freedom. His desire is to deliver us from hindrances and to free us for advancement!

God's plan is progressing. The path ahead is formed, and we must choose to take our place on that path so that His glory can be revealed through our surrendered lives. It's time to go forward. God is calling us! But we MUST listen for His sound and respond to His drawing! God is restoring us to life. He is awakening us to position us so that He can work through us. It's a whole new dimension of glory and power that He is requiring us to experience and demonstrate in this moment.

The Spinning is Turning

I received an encouraging vision and word from the Lord.

In the vision, I saw people, who I knew were members of the Body of Christ, and they were spinning around very swiftly like a top when it has been released from the string. Off to the side, I could see the enemy watching them and laughing and mocking. Suddenly, I saw the finger of God being placed on the heads of these people, and the spinning stopped. And in that moment, they began to glow with a brilliant light!

Immediately, I heard the Lord say, "The nauseating dizziness and all of the confusion from the unexpected attacks that have been launched against you has come to an end!"

Then He said, "The attacks have not created a weakness! In spite of what the enemy tried to do, I have strengthened your spirit man, and what I have developed in you will now begin to radiate through you with a fervency that cannot be extinguished or avoided! Healing and strength are your portion! You are stepping out of a dark, spinning season into the light of My 'now' moment, and as you walk with Me, I will shine through you with power and the manifestation of My might! The spinning is now becoming a 'turning of events'...a turning in your favor!"

At another time, the Lord said to me, "I have built in you a resistance that hell cannot penetrate! You are fortified. The barrier that is formed around you will not hem you in; it will keep hell out! I Am surrounding you as a wall of fire, and My glory is in you to flow for you and out through you in magnificent ways!"

One day I was praying, and out of my mouth came rushing these words: "The love of God is powerful! The blood of Jesus is all-powerful! The power of God is unmatched! I am surrounded by and hidden within all three, and that is a shield that is impenetrable!"

Over the past few years, there has been an undeniable increase of an onslaught of spiritual resistance that has been experienced by the praying church. BUT Holy Spirit has put us in remembrance of this unchangeable truth: greater is He that is in us than any force of hell that comes against us! We are surrounded by an impenetrable force of the power of God. Though the battle has been intense, our assurance is that we are fortified and hell cannot defeat us. No amount of resistance will stop us as God works through us to fulfill His intentions for this nation! Now the spinning is ending, and things are turning as the Ancient of days rises on our behalf.

Be assured that your labor in the Lord has not been in vain! Your prayers and obedience have mattered, and now God is turning things. He has put His finger on us, and we will now rise with a greater intensity and radiance of His manifested Glory!

I feel the Lord is saying:

Your relentless and persistent pursuit has captured the attention of Heaven. My eyes have run to and fro to find hearts that are turned toward Me. I have found such hearts in you, and now I will begin to show Myself strong on your behalf. This is a divine moment. Stay the course. Don't get entrapped by your emotions. Don't relax your stand on what I have said! My Word stands! Do not allow weariness to rob you of your due season! Don't lose hope, and don't discard your courage! I Am re-adjusting your vision and stabilizing your resolve. You will run and not grow weary! Shake off the dizziness. Reorganize for renewed activity. Be re-energized to mobilize! Onward is your command!

Revitalized to Mobilize

Dutch Sheets recently said, "It's time for the Ekklesia to step up. This is our time. Do not grow weary now! Grab hold of that surge, that second wind that comes to an athlete, and he says, 'I see the finish line. I feel adrenaline flowing inside me! I'm ready to do this!'"

I believe we are in a time when God is re-sensitizing us. The weariness of the last season has dulled us, somewhat, to our ability and even to our desire to really hear Him. But in this time, He is opening us up, and He is refilling us with the Oil of His Spirit. We will now begin to feel His nearness, and we will find ourselves being drawn to Him, maybe even like we haven't felt in years. Many have lost their passion, and they don't even realize it! But as He pours His Spirit over us, there is an awakening of passion for Him that is going to transpire in us, and we are going to be amazed by the newness of hunger we will have for Him and by the clarity of hearing that will return. As we step under the refreshing flow of Holy Spirit, we will draw near to Him, and the fire of our passion for Him will be rekindled. We are going to be re-sensitized to His voice. We are going to hear Him again! The Body of Christ will be revitalized to mobilize.

God is awakening and "re-life-ing" the Body. He's assembling the parts so that we function in the fullness and demonstration of His power. He's giving us strategy and revelation for positioning and assignments. Some of the assignments we receive may take us out of our comfort zone and require us to do things we've never done before. We will more than likely be stretched beyond what we feel we are capable. Yet, we will find that He has already anointed and prepared us for the work that is to be done.

Prayer is a key element for us in this time. Jesus, Himself modeled this for us in His earthly ministry. Prayer connects us to God, and it is the vehicle through which He reveals to us His will. It is also through deep times of intercession that He allows us to hear His wisdom and then become a conduit through which He can speak forth His wisdom to set things into motion that are necessary for the unfolding of particular parts of His plan. It's time for us to once again pray those "effectual and fervent prayers" that provoke things to move in alignment with the plan of God in the earth.

Those effectual, fervent prayers are not just last-minute attempts to somehow hopefully get God to move. They are prayers that flow from the heart of unwavering faith that has been established by abiding in the Lord's presence. As we draw near to Him in the place of His presence, we hear His Word and His will, and we are provoked to speak and align ourselves in agreement with Him for His will to happen.

Don't become so entrapped by the emotions that have been influenced by the experiences of the previous seasons. Stay focused on the Lord. The journey is not finished. There is more, and the Lord is putting His finger on us to stop the spin and allow us to refocus and regain our stability in Him so that we can run forward to accomplish every purpose for which He is sending us.

I feel there is an increase that is coming to those who will respond in faith and obedience to the Lord in this moment—an increase of strength, vision, and spiritual perception, an increase of wisdom and strategy. God is taking us to another level of seeing and hearing in and by the Spirit. He is increasing our awareness of the authority we have in our speaking and praying. Our confidence in Him is increasing. Our boldness is increasing. And we will remain steadfast at our post and watch as Holy Spirit works through our obedience to set things in motion so that the Word of the Lord is activated to accomplish His purposes and intentions.

I hear a clarion call echoing from the throne room of God to the heart of His true warriors:

Shake off distractions.
Shake off disappointment.
Rise! Take your place. Set your face like a flint toward Me. Stand! Do not be moved by what you see happening around you! It's temporary. It will not last always. There is a turning in the works. I have told you ahead of time, and now is the time! Believe My promises. Remember My Word! DO NOT DOUBT IT!

God has risen on our behalf. The spinning is becoming a turning of events. Things are turning in our favor, and with a renewed ability to focus, we will continue to work with Holy Spirit as He leads us according to the will of the Father.

We are being transitioned from the process of becoming into the position of being, so there is a stirring and movement that is happening in the Body—an awakening, a movement.

When the Body that we are a part of begins to move, it forces all of the parts to have to move with it. Sometimes the stress that we feel is created by our own hesitation to move and to do our part when it's time.

We are stepping out of a dark, spinning season into the light of this redemptive moment. The nauseating dizziness, as well as all of the confusion, has come to an end. We are getting our focus back, and we will now rise as a prepared people, ready to move into this prepared moment with a greater intensity and radiance of God's manifested glory!

It's our time! We're up! He's called us to attention. This is what it's all been about. Everything God has done has led us to this moment. His hand is good upon us, and we are well able to possess all that He has promised. It's happening, and Jesus is saying to His Body, "Don't hesitate to take your place!"

In a recent gathering, the Lord spoke the following word through me to His Church:

> A wrong focus has allowed an amplification of the voice of the enemy, and the voice of the enemy has been influencing your emotions. But your Dread Champion has risen up for you to see Him and to capture your focus. As you focus on your Dread Champion, He, the all-consuming fire, is burning the bridges behind you so that you will not be tempted to cross back over in an effort to deal with the false burdens that the enemy has confined you to in past seasons.

The Lord is untethering us from false obligations to false burdens that have been erected by the voice of the enemy. The only weapon the enemy has is a lie. The only way the lie works is if you believe it. The only way you will believe the lie is if you don't know, understand, and believe and keep before you the truth of God's Word.

If you feel a lack of confidence trying to invade your mind, causing you to feel insignificant and incapable, see those things for what they are: restricting lies of the enemy! Do not allow those deceptions to sabotage your destiny. Do not allow them to override your faith in God! Resist those thoughts and quickly bring them captive to the obedience of Christ! You can do this! You have already been prepared!

Let's pray this prayer together:

Father, thank You for bringing the spin to an end and for turning things in our favor. You have broken the snare, and we are escaped from hell's attempt to stop us. We refuse to allow evil agendas to talk us into surrendering our post. We shake off the dizziness of the last season, and we take our steadfast stand as Your watchmen on the wall. Thank You for healing us physically, mentally, emotionally, and spiritually so that with renewed focus and strength we can rise to finish what You have started in and through us! We trust You, and we will not be afraid. You are our strength and our defense, and You are our Salvation. Your favor is upon us, and You will establish the work of our hands. We breathe in Your awakening breath, and we shout with steadfast resolve, "Weariness will not rob us of our due season!" You, O, Lord, will satisfy us with Your mercy, and we will rejoice and be glad, for we shall see the performance of those things that You have said and shown to us in prayer! Amen!

8

Anchored in Hope

This hope [this confident assurance] we have as an anchor of the soul [it cannot slip and it cannot break down under whatever pressure bears upon it]—a safe and steadfast hope.

Hebrews 6:19 AMP

IN THIS URGENT TIME, THE BODY OF CHRIST *is* awakening. The beneficiaries of His amazing spiritual inheritance are realizing the unlimited resources that have been made available to us as the Father's heirs. If we seek Him, we will find Him. If we knock, the door will be opened to us. If we ask, we will receive (see Matthew 7:7-8).

Through the dreams, visions, prophetic words, and scriptural insights that we have discussed throughout the pages of this book, we are left with the understanding that our lives matter to God. Through us, He desires to reveal the reality of His power and Person to all mankind. He loves us, and through our acceptance of Christ as Savior, He has made us His very own children. The time has come for us to discover the full benefits of our spiritual inheritance and to be transformed by the full appropriation of its intended purposes. Jesus Christ has established us to be the Ekklesia, members of His Body, functioning in alignment with His leading as the Head. He works through us to do the will of God and to demonstrate the manifestation of His Kingdom power and authority. He's calling us to receive all that He has made available, to dare to believe Him, and to humble ourselves to walk with—and work with—Him. Filled with His Spirit and clothed in His righteousness, we must put on the whole armor of God. We must watch and imitate Him as He works through us to reveal His power and to keep things in timing and right alignment with His eternal plan.

Much is happening as this great awakening has begun and continues to unfold. We rejoice for the movement that we have seen, but we must not become slack and complacent. The door is open; now advancement must be made. We know that what we have seen is only the beginning. There is more to come, and in this time, we must be attentive and instantly and completely obedient to His voice so that through us His will is done in our time…and for the sake of those who will come after us!

Work While You Celebrate

In February of this year, I had a very detailed dream that reveals strategy and instructions for the next several months and for the future. It reveals to us that God is serious about His original intentions for the Church and for our nation. While I do not yet understand all of the symbolism, I do know that Holy Spirit will give us personal and corporate clarity for assignments and events that will need to be carried out in the days ahead. I ask that you not just read through the dream, but pray. Pray about your part. Pray for the Church. Pray for the heirs to rise with revelation of their spiritual authority and, with undaunted determination, to take our place, release our supply, and see His Kingdom come!

> I dreamed that thousands of people had been summoned by the Lord to gather in a certain place. I am not sure where this place was located, but we were

112

gathered in a very large coliseum-type building. The seating was sloped downward, and the stage was at the bottom of the slope. There were thousands of people in the seats, and on the stage were hundreds of people sitting in chairs. I knew that the people in the auditorium were born-again believers from all around America, and the people on the stage were Christian leaders: leaders of businesses, ministries, churches, denominations, colleges and schools, political leaders, etc.

As we all took our seats, suddenly, there was a huge overhead screen that appeared. Everyone in the entire building, no matter where they were seated, had the ability to see it.

On the screen was a map of the United States. On the map, we began to see these geyser-type eruptions popping up in various cities. The first one was near Lexington, Kentucky. We knew this represented what was happening, at that time, at Asbury University. Then other "geysers" began to pop up on the map. When the "geysers" erupted, they would spew out fire, water, and oil that would immediately saturate the areas surrounding them. This was all happening in real time. We were literally watching the move of God, as it was quickly spreading to the nation. There was a thunderous applause and celebration that started to spread throughout the coliseum as we watched this happening on the map.

As the celebration broke out, suddenly, the voice of God resounded. It was like His voice came down out of the heavens through a sound system, and it sounded like loud, deep thunder. It created a vibration that we could literally feel as it shook the floor beneath us.

He said very adamantly, *"Do NOT become distracted by the movement!"*

You could then hear a collective gasp released from the crowd. We all wondered, "What does that mean? What is He saying?"

He continued, *"Celebrate the movement, YES! But do not become distracted by it!* **Work while you celebrate!***"* He repeated that statement three or four times, and it gripped us deeply. It was like a jolt that readjusted our focus. There was great joy for what was beginning to happen, but in that moment, we all became captured by a sense of urgency. It was then that we realized this was not a "normal" gathering. This was an urgent call to attention.

As those real-time happenings continued to show on the map on the overhead screen, there were two MASSIVE, steel cable ropes that dropped down onto the stage in front of those leaders seated there. Each of these cables had a very large steel ring on either end— so, two cables and four rings.

As soon as those cables hit the stage, four angels suddenly appeared. The angels took hold of the cables and carried them out from our location. After a few seconds, we could then see the angels—with the cables—on that overhead screen. The angels worked in pairs. Two of them carried one cable, each holding a ring in their hands. One angel went north to an anchor that was located there. The anchor was something that had already been set in place. It was very old, and it went deep into the ground. The angel placed the ring over that anchor, securing his end of the cable in place. The other angel took his ring south to an anchor that was located there and placed the ring over that anchor and secured his end of the cable in place.

The other two angels went east and west, and in those locations, they placed the rings that were on the ends of the cable over anchors situated there and secured the cable in place.

When this was completed, two more cables fell onto the stage in front of those leaders. Immediately the four angels returned and did as before. This time, two angels took one cable and placed the rings over anchors that were in place in the northwest and southeast, securing the cable in place. The other cable was secured from anchors in a northeast and a southwest location.

Now, on the screen, we were looking at the map through the crisscross of these four cables that had been anchored in place.

Then the Lord said, *"There is a shaking that is coming, but you must not fear! You must know and be convinced that this nation is anchored and surrounded. KNOW that! Be convinced of that!"*

Next, there appeared a manilla folder in the lap of each of the leaders who were seated on the stage. We each opened our folder to find one sheet of paper. On the paper were listed four instructive bullet points. Across the top of the page was written: COMMAND THE FOREWORD!

When I read those words, I was a bit confused. The phrase was not "Command the Forward," as in advancement; it read, "Command the Foreword." I understood that a foreword is something written for the beginning of a book. Was He saying that everything was going to be destroyed by this "shaking" that He had said was coming and that a "new book" was going to be started for America?

There was a microphone on the stage, and I worked up enough courage to walk up to it and ask, "Lord, what does this mean?"

He answered audibly, speaking to us all in that coliseum, "*It's time to command what was written at the beginning. Command the foreword! Bring this nation back into alignment with that which was written in the beginning—when this land became a nation. It's the purposes for which She was established. Those prophetic decrees were spoken in the beginning in agreement with My intended purposes. Now, I say to you, COMMAND THE FOREWORD! Know My purposes! Decree those purposes! Do not back down! Know what I have said and established. Agree and decree in agreement with Me, and your decrees will provoke a shaking that will bring this nation back into alignment with My original 'Foreword.'*"

In that moment, the place where we were gathered began to vibrate with what felt like an electrical current. A wind started to blow, and then it was as if fire just dropped down out of the heavens onto every one of us. It wasn't a natural, flaming fire; it was the fiery presence of the Lord as He entered that room in a visible, tangible demonstration. When that happened, people began falling into the floor, overwhelmed by the presence of the Lord. Some fell to their knees and began to weep. Others were running around, lifting their hands with shouts of joy!

The thing that came to my mind in that moment was, *"This is a true baptism of Fire!"* And none in that room was exempt from it. No one questioned or debated it. No one was offended by the reactions to it! No one said, "We don't believe in this!" or "This is not how we do it at our church!" This baptism of fire came with force and, everyone received it! Somehow, we all understood that we were being transformed by the Fire of God.

After some time, the leaders and all of those in the room were able to sit back down in their seats. As we each took our seat, a paint brush and a bucket filled with oil appeared at every person's feet. The Lord instructed us, *"Go from here. Carry the Oil and secure the perimeters of your states. Paint the perimeters with the Oil, and it will be secured."* We knew He was showing us that this, too, will help to secure us when the shaking comes.

Then the attention of each of the leaders was drawn back to the piece of paper that was in our folders. We began to look at and discuss each of the bullet points that were listed.

The first bullet point said: "Get it anchored! Anchor the nation." Beside that point was a red check mark, meaning that this point had already been completed. We had just witnessed the completion of this point as the angels secured those steel cables to the anchors.

The second point said: "Secure the perimeters of all fifty states. Get the perimeters painted with the Oil!" We knew this was why we had been given the buckets of oil and the paint brushes.

The third bullet point said: "Establish an anchor in each state and connect it to the guide wire." We all understood this to mean that each state must be anchored and connected to the cables, which the angels had secured to the anchors on the outer perimeters of the nation. The Lord was now referring to these cables as the "guide wire."

The last point said: "Establish a prayer grid in each state." We understood this to mean that prayer teams were to be to established in each state. There must be a grid of prayer teams, connected groups of people who are listening in prayer and ready to move quickly with any assignments the Lord would give.

Throughout the entire dream, the map was still on the screen, and the fire pockets were continuing to erupt in real time. There were many of these eruptions that popped up—first, in the eastern part of the nation, then slowly they began to pop up throughout the whole nation.

The Lord then instructed all of us to get into groups. Most of the people were grouped according to the states where they lived. These would be sent back to their state to watch in prayer and to carry out specific assignments that had to do with the bullet points listed on the page we had been given. So, there were fifty state groups formed.

Then others were assigned to regions. There were four of these groups formed. These would watch in prayer and be able to facilitate and assist in assignments that had to do with the state groups located within their region.

Then another group was formed that would be assigned to the entire nation. These would watch in prayer and be able to facilitate and assist in assignments that had to do with the regional groups, as well as all of the state groups.

As we each got into our group, everyone stood, holding the bucket of oil and the paint brush we had been given. We knew that our first priority was to get the perimeters "painted" with the Oil, and this must be done quickly.

Then on the overhead screen, there was a calendar that was laid over the top of the map. It was not a calendar with one month and its days; it was one page showing all twelve months with their days. On that page, the month of September was circled in red ink. We then saw the finger of God on the screen, tapping the month of September on that calendar. As we saw this, we again felt that rush of urgency, realizing that God was showing to us that there was not a lot of time to get everything done.

There was excitement for the "eruptions" that have already taken place, but there was also a deep knowing that this was just a beginning. There was still much that needed to be established, and we were being "sent" by the Lord to do the work.

That was the end of the dream.

I am not going to attempt to interpret this entire dream. As I mentioned earlier, I think that it is so important for each of us to pray for personal revelation and understanding so that we have true clarity and instruction from the Lord concerning our part in this assignment of commanding His original "foreword." However, I will share some insights for the dream that I feel are important for all of us, as the corporate Body of Christ, to understand.

Let me start by addressing the circling of the month of September on the calendar. I do not believe that this was a prophetic warning about the month of September. I do not know what will unfold in the months ahead. I believe the month was circled as a sign from the Lord to the Body of Christ that we must work diligently to complete those bullet points and any additional assignments that He will reveal to us by that time. For some reason, the month of September was important. I do not have any prophetic insight at this time as to what that may be. However, I do know that what God is doing now will not end in September, but what we do now, in obedience to the Lord, *will* have a profound impact on strengthening and securing the Church for all that unfolds both now and in the future.

We must settle in our minds the indisputable fact that God has not led us to this point in time for the purpose of allowing everything He has said and done to just crumble and fall to nothing. He sees the end from the beginning. He has already looked over into the end of time and of all things and begun the work to put everything in place so that His ultimate end-time goal will be completed. Every generation has been equipped and led by God to fulfill their particular part of His plan that had to do with each of their times. As each part was completed, the next part was set into motion. The common thread woven through every generation is the spiritual inheritance that He imparts to all who will believe on Him and humble themselves to walk with Him. He has given us access into His fullness, enabling us to hear, receive, and be empowered to effectively and successfully do our part.

In the dream, God made it clear that He has never forgotten the purposes that He has had for America since before She was even established. He referred to these purposes as His "original foreword." Our true history records that an idea and a longing began to stir in the hearts of a group of men and women in the nation of England, as God placed in them a longing for a homeland where they could be free to live their lives productively and worship Him without restriction. That desire provoked them to eventually leave everything they had known, and taking huge leaps of faith, they set out on a long, arduous and uncertain journey of discovery.

That journey led them to the eastern shores of what would become one of the greatest nations on the earth. Her greatness would not be because the people did everything right—many dark moments have been recorded throughout our history. Her greatness would be because She was established as a nation "under God." He led those pilgrims to these shores, and upon their landing, they planted a cross on that beach, and through them, God prophesied His intentions for Her existence.

On April 29, 1607, Reverend Robert Hunt stood and offered this prayer:

> We do hereby dedicate this Land and ourselves to reach the people within these shores with the Gospel of Jesus Christ and to raise up Godly generations after us, and with these generations, take the Kingdom of God to all the earth. May this covenant of dedication remain to all generations as long as this earth remains,

and may this land, along with England, be Evangelist to the world. May all who see this cross remember what we have done here, and may those, who come here to inhabit, join us in this covenant and in this most noble work that the Holy Scriptures may be fulfilled. From these very shores, the Gospel shall go forth, not only to this New World, but the entire world.

The following Bible passage was then read at the conclusion of his prayer.

All the ends of the world shall remember and turn to the Lord, and all the kindreds of the nations shall worship before Thee. For the Kingdom is the Lord's, and He ruleth among the nations.

Psalm 22:27-28, Geneva Bible

While I do not fully understand the symbolism and location of the anchors to which the angels secured the nation in the dream, I am sure that the cross they planted on that beach on April 29, 1607, marked one of them. As Robert Hunt released that prophetic prayer, right then and there, God revealed His purpose for the United States of America. From those words, we can conclude that at the very founding of this nation, God was deeply anchoring Her to His prophetic declaration, "America shall be saved!"

Though She has rocked and reeled in the tempest winds of evil agendas—and at times it has seemed She would surely fall—America still stands! She stands because God has purpose for this nation! He has never forgotten nor abandoned His original desires for Her establishment. His plan has not failed. His Word has not been altered!

Throughout America's history, there have always been those who have held fast to the Lord and to His original purposes. God has seen to it that the people within these shores have been reached with the Gospel of Jesus Christ, enabling godly generations to be raised up after them, and through them, the Gospel has been, and continues to be, sent out from here. Through the years, thousands have devoted their lives to take His message to the nations of the world. In every generation, He secured a remnant of people, who believed on Him and were saved by grace through faith in Jesus Christ, enabling this spiritual inheritance to be carried on.

Now the fruit of the godly seeds that have been sown in previous generations is ripe, and the time of harvest has come. It is a harvest of the harvesters, and God is beckoning us to see, to hear, and to be reminded that He has always had a plan and a purpose! As members of Christ's Body, we have been led into this moment on purpose for His purpose.

Our nation is once again rocking and reeling in the adverse winds that are being stirred as evil agendas have been set into place to seek to uproot the anchors and destroy the foundation of our nation's Christian heritage. All around the world, sin is abounding and from a natural perspective, it seems that evil will surely prevail…but it will not happen!

God has summoned the Ekklesia. He is calling the Body of Christ to attention. I believe the Church, in America and worldwide, is experiencing a re-awakening to an awareness of God, and He is marking those, who will respond to His drawing in this season, with a true baptism of fire! He is filling us afresh with His Spirit and with revelation of all that belongs to us as His heirs. He is igniting us with a deeper passion for Him and to see His original purposes to be fulfilled.

Yeshua is positioning the members of His Body, and we must each take our place and give heed to His instructions. A shaking is coming, but He has secured us to the anchor. We must know that and be convinced of that! He has surrounded us with the hosts of Heaven, who have been sent at His command to assist us both now and in the days ahead.

Movement has already begun. Pockets of revival and awakening are beginning to spring forth, releasing the refreshing waters of the Word of God and of the transforming power of the Oil and Fire of the Spirit. It's happening now, and for that, we greatly rejoice! But as we see what God has done and is doing, we must not allow ourselves to be so captivated by what has started that we think that He is done! Celebrate? Yes! How can you not, when we see lives changed, bodies being healed, hearts being restored, and Jesus being sought after with sincere hunger and desire to know Him for real? Yes, we celebrate, but we must not become distracted by what has been started as though that's all there is! We must work while we celebrate! We work in cooperation with Holy Spirit as He leads us and announces to us in detail the things that are yet to be done, and then we must obey Him completely as He instructs us in what we must do.

One of the things He told us to do in the dream was to establish a prayer grid in each state. Jesus is calling the Church to refocus on Him. He is connecting the Body. He is joining the parts so that we can each release our supply and work together with Him in prayer and assignments that He will make known to us. We must listen as He reveals His will to us and then pray and declare His will to be done! Respond when He tells us things to do. Use that key of faith in God to unlock what He is desiring to be unlocked. Allow that faith to provoke in us an undaunted obedience to Him. If He says pray, then we must pray under the direction of Holy Spirit as He leads us. If He says go, then we must go wherever He sends us. If He says give, then give. If He says witness, then we will witness to those to whom He will lead us. If He says write a book, then write a book. If He says start a business, then start a business. Whatever He tells us to do, we must do it without hesitation. As we humble ourselves to walk and work with Him, we are strengthening our cords of connection to Him so that we can:

> *Hold tightly to the hope set before us. This hope [this confident assurance] we have* **as an anchor** *of the soul [it cannot slip and it cannot break down under whatever pressure bears upon it]—a safe and steadfast hope.*

Hebrews 6:18-19 AMP (emphasis mine)

We are anchored in hope, and that Hope has a name: Jesus! He is the secure and steadfast anchor of our souls! As we place our complete trust in Him, we will follow as He leads, not only securing ourselves to Him as our anchor, but we also become a vessel through which Holy Spirit will work to impact our territories. Jesus declared, *"The Spirit of the Lord is upon Me because He has* **anointed** *Me"* (Luke 4:18, emphasis mine). As heirs of salvation, when the Spirit of the Lord comes upon us, we receive the same anointing that was upon Jesus, which enabled Him to release the power of God everywhere He went. It is very interesting that the word anointed in this Scripture is the Hebrew word *mashach*, which means "to rub with oil, to anoint; by implication, it also means to consecrate; **to paint**" (Strong's Definitions). Jesus has painted us with the oil of His anointing, which enables us to release decrees, prayers, and acts of obedience to God with such power and authority that we paint and smear our homes, our churches, our schools, our businesses, the marketplace, our regions, our territories, our states, our nations with the oil of His Spirit as He flows through us! In one sense, we each become His paintbrush! This is why we cannot quench Holy Spirit by hesitating to obey His promptings. When we allow Him to work through us, the anointing flows, and power is released to paint the atmosphere with the evidence of the transforming glory of God.

Influence a Nation with Revival

The operation of Holy Ghost power in and through our lives will further secure our perimeters because evil cannot resist—nor overpower—the anointing! Dwight Moody rightly stated, "The work of the Spirit is to impart life, to implant hope, to give liberty, to testify of Christ, to guide us into all truth, to teach us all things, to comfort the believer, and to convict the world of sin." When the Church returns to a true passionate pursuit of the Lord, we will once again be enlightened with the revelation of our calling and purpose in Him. As we take our place in that calling and purpose, Holy Spirit will work through us to restore the demonstration of the power of God that will provoke an unstoppable awakening to an awareness of God. This is why we exist. My friend, Pastor Kim Owens, says, "We exist to influence a nation with revival!"

How do we influence a nation with revival? When we walk in obedience to the Lord, we become sowers of His righteous seeds! Through every act of obedience to the Lord, we are releasing a supply of the anointing that will provoke a righteous harvest that will transform our territories.

My daddy was a farmer. When he would prepare the garden each spring, he didn't just till the ground and wait for a harvest. He released the supply that he had—he planted seeds. Once those seeds were sown, they had the power to grow and transform that field of dirt into a garden of abundance.

The apostle Paul said, *"God is able to make all grace abound to you so that, always having all sufficiency in everything, you may have an abundance for every good deed...Now He Who supplies seed to the sower and bread for food will supply and multiply your seed for sowing and increase the harvest of your righteousness"* (2 Corinthians 9:8, 10 NASB).

In this portion of scripture, Paul is literally referring to our giving, but I do believe his words are also applicable to what God is speaking to us in this moment. As those around us are influenced by the reality of Jesus as He reaches through us to make Himself known, reviving will happen! Change will come. Light will dispel the darkness, giving those who are blinded by the god of this world the opportunity to see and to hear truth that has the power to liberate them from the strongholds of deception. Lives will be changed. More glory-carriers will be awakened and rightly positioned to sow these seeds of obedience to God that will yield a harvest of transformation and righteousness.

This is the time that we must appeal to Heaven, not just for the purpose of petitioning for our wants and desires, but for the purpose of hearing God's desires and His instructions for us so that we can work with Him to fulfill those desires. The days ahead are crucial. We cannot be influenced by what is happening around us; we should be influencing what is happening around us! As we hear the instructions from the Lord and follow those instructions, we will raise the Standard that will turn the tide of evil.

There is excitement for the "eruptions" that have already taken place, but there is also a deep knowing that this is just a beginning. There is still much that needs to be established, and we are being "sent" by the Lord to do the work. From this point forward, we should approach each day with the understanding that God has already looked out over that day and that He declares, "I know the plans that I have for you." The intent of our heart should then be that of hearing those plans and humbly responding, "Here am I, Lord. Send me." This is how we become imitators of Christ. Through prayer, we are able to hear and see what the Father desires, and, by faith, we become hearers and doers of His divine will!

To those who are ready and willing to work with Him to establish His original foreword, the Lord is saying:

> You have entered a place of releasing divine purpose and destiny! Things will begin to unfold that will surprise you and even cause you to ask, 'God, what *is* this?' And you will find signs that will alert you to the fact that you are indeed in a new place. But do not fear, for I will guide you! Don't follow your emotions; they are not trustworthy. Follow Me as I order your steps. Listen for My instructions and free yourself to obey Me instantly. Focus forward, not behind, and not self-ward. There is much to get done. I Am fulfilling My Word for this time. This is a vital moment, and I need you to stay alert. Watch Me. Trust Me. Obey Me. Work with Me.

> Divine connections are about to be made. Ways are opening! Ideas are coming! There are prayers you prayed, thinking they were for the moment in which you prayed them, but I provoked those prayers ahead of time to set into motion things meant for this time. There are courses of events that have been working together to form this moment. Now, you are entering the door of your "defining moment," and things will begin to happen very quickly. Stay above the fray so you can hear and see from My perspective. Move with instant obedience as I lead you forward!

9

In His Grip

*Because I, your God, have a firm grip on you and I'm not letting
go. I'm telling you, 'Don't panic. I'm right here to help you.'*

Isaiah 43:13 MSG

ONE OF MY FAVORITE ACCOUNTS RECORDED in the Bible is that
of the nation of Israel's crossing of the Jordan River into the
land of promise. Joshua had been positioned by the Lord to lead
the people forward. He had received from the Lord the mantle
of a leadership position that had previously been held and worn
by Moses. As he stepped into that history-making moment,
Joshua did so with a command and a promise from the Lord.

> *As I was with Moses, so I will be with you. I will not leave you
> nor forsake you. Be strong and of good courage; do not be afraid,
> nor be dismayed; for the Lord your God is with you wherever you
> go.*

Joshua 1:5b, 9 NKJV

The time had come for them to possess the land, just as God
had promised Moses.

Moses had led the people out of Egyptian bondage. Burning
with the fervency of the provocation of the Lord, Moses had

assumed the role of leadership, and though he may not have done everything right, he did his part in his time. He and all of the people witnessed, time and time again, the undeniable evidence of God's presence with them and His power to keep them: the parting of the Red Sea, a visible cloud by day and a column of fire by night to lead them, supernatural provision of food and water, and their clothes and shoes did not wear out in forty years of consistent wilderness travel. They witnessed the protection of God from their enemies and the finger of God writing His laws on stone tablets. God had not only led them out of bondage, which was, in and of itself, a miracle, but He continued to daily lead them supernaturally, every step of the way.

Moses and his generation received the initial revealing of this promise from God, along with an assurance of His sincerity and intentions to fulfill it. And with every supernatural act of God, every intervention, and every act of provision, the inheritance was maturing and growing. Their obedience to make that journey is what set things into motion for the inheritance to be passed along. Now, they had come to the time when the next part of the plan would be revealed and unlocked. Everything they had done and witnessed up to that point had enabled the next generation to not only know about the promise but also to receive the inheritance and carry it on with courage and a confident knowing that God was surely with them.

By the time Joshua and the people received the baton to carry on with the next leg of the journey, the weight of the mantle had greatly increased. Now, it was no longer just the promise they passed along, it was the promise accompanied by the stories, the events that gave them undeniable evidence, and the testimony of God's ability and willingness to assist them as they took their place on the timeline of His plan.

The inheritance had been given to them by promise, and the fulfillment of that promise was waiting just across the Jordan River. It was their time to carry on with the promise. God had given the assurance that He would do for Joshua and his generation everything that He did for Moses and the generation before them—and even greater!

The crossing of the Jordan, at any other time, would have been uneventful, but this was the harvest season, and the torrential rains had run down from the plateaus, causing the river to flood. This means that the flood waters were greatly complicating their advancement, but they had a promise and a command from the Lord to go over that river and possess the land. In that moment, the testimonies of the previous generation were shouting to this generation of the goodness and power of God. God was, in essence, saying to Joshua, "It's your time to wear the mantle. Moses wore it for his time, and he has left you with the evidence that I Am is well able to keep you and lead you on. As I was with Moses, I will be with you." The assurance that came from the testimonies of the power of God that were passed down to Joshua gave him an uncommon courage to lead the people over that flooded river in order to advance the inheritance for generations yet to come.

I can only imagine the feeling of awe and reverence for the Lord that must have rushed through them when the waters of that Jordan parted and stood up in a heap upstream, creating for them a dry path to the other side. I'm sure they must have exclaimed, "It's true! The testimonies—the stories that our ancestors passed down to us—are all true! God *is* all-powerful, and He *is* with us!" The relief and confirmation must have been overwhelming. They were receiving their inheritance and the undeniable revelation that God truly had every intention to do all that He had promised!

As they crossed the Jordan, Joshua commanded them to gather twelve stones from the midst of the river and build a memorial. This memorial was not for the purpose of saying that what they were doing would have to one day be done again. It wasn't a road marker; those stones were to be a reminder for the "children of Israel forever" (Joshua 4:7). Those stones were a testimony of the power of God and His love and ability to guide all who will trust in Him. They were a witness for all to see and know that God is serious about His promises!

Some people say that we don't need all of that "old stuff" anymore. They wrongly preach that we just need to forget all of that and start fresh and new. We are in a new season, but this new season is somewhat tied to the old season. What was done in obedience to God by those in past generations has made it possible for us to receive and carry on with the purposes of God for our times. The truth is, if those who have gone before us had not done their part, you and I could not do our part. Think about that! They may not have done everything right—and everything they passed along to us wasn't part of the inheritance that God intended—but many of them did their part for their time, and they experienced and demonstrated the provisions of our spiritual inheritance. They left us a witness that enables us to not only know about the promise, but also to receive the inheritance and carry it on with boldness and courage and confident faith in God. We can advance with the assurance that as He was with them, He is with us! We are assured that the powerful things that God did for and through them, He can and will do all of that and even greater for and through us as we take our place in His purposes.

The Book of Acts, the Welsh Revival, the outpouring in the mountains of Tennessee and North Carolina, the Azusa Street Revival, the great revivals in the Hebrides, the Red River and

Cane Ridge revivals, the Pensacola and Toronto Outpourings, and all of the moves of God throughout history...these are *our* memorial stones. They are not indicators of events that have to be recreated, but rather, these are witnesses that shout to our generation the reminder that we have an inheritance. They remind us that God is real, Jesus is real, and Holy Spirit is real! These events and the lives of those who lived before us are witnesses that declare to us that, as the heirs of God and joint-heirs with Christ, we have been given an inheritance that enables us to be living carriers of the fullness of the reality of the Godhead in our physical bodies in order to reveal the reality of their power and presence to the world!

There is never a need for any generation to suffer from spiritual poverty. Tucked away in our lineage is an inheritance that is extremely valuable, and its value has never faded. The reality of its existence and content must be experienced by each generation *and passed along* with even greater weight and impact to those who are yet to come.

The inheritance is not about age; it's not just the older passing things on to the younger. It's about all of us taking God at His word and allowing Him to reveal the fullness of Who He is in and through our lives.

For Joshua, Moses' life wasn't an outdated part of history that was no longer necessary and relevant for him. His life was a testimony that gave Joshua the courage to carry on and do his part. When they crossed the Jordan River and went in to possess the land, it wasn't just the young generation that was advancing, it was a united effort of young and old. Though many did die in the wilderness, still Joshua and Caleb were among those that carried on. They had been with Moses. They had even been in the Promised Land as spies, whom Moses sent to investigate the land. They were forerunners of the promise, and it was their faith in God and His abilities that enabled them to go forward when others retreated. Caleb was eighty-five years old, and His declaration was, "Give me my portion!" He refused to be the point in the family line where the inheritance would be breached. He intended for those who followed him to receive what rightfully belonged to them as heirs!

We have entered a significant moment on the timeline of God's plan, and what we do in this moment will determine whether or not we experience the fullness of God's intentions for our time. Young and old, we are here in this time, and we have purpose in God. We must claim our portion and refuse to live in spiritual poverty! We must know, believe, and receive by faith the promise of the inheritance of God's fullness so that its reality can be demonstrated through our lives! We must do our part for our time—and our time is now!

Chuck Pierce has taught us that God is not in time the way we are, but God is working His plan, and where His plan is concerned, He knows the exact second on the timeline on which He is working. I believe that on the timeline of God's plan, there come certain moments that are timely, defining moments. These are the moments that make us or break us.

Defining moments are also decision moments. It's kind of similar to the moment when the executor reads the will; the inheritance is being revealed, and the heirs have to choose to believe and receive it or deny and walk away from it. We are the heirs, and our Heavenly Father is saying, "I have given you an inheritance. I have given you My Word and countless witnesses to reveal it to you. What will you do with that which I have given?" What we choose to do in this moment has the power to determine our future and the future of the generations to come.

Creation is groaning for the manifestation of the sons and daughters of God. Our nation and the nations of the world are in a time of crisis. Souls hang in the balance. The prophetic destiny of our nation is being weighed in the balance. The Lord showed to me that, for a time, righteousness and evil will be running parallel, both making great strides for their causes, but a shift is soon coming. A shaking is on the horizon. Many have already begun to feel the intensity of the transition. But we must not fear! Evil will not prevail. God assures us that He is still seated on His throne, and He says, "My reign remains!" We can trust Him. We can be confident that He always knows what He is doing and that He is well able to guide us! The shaking may prove to be intense in the days ahead, and at times, it may seem that all is lost, but we cannot cast away our confidence in Him. When the dust settles and the fog lifts, we will find that He never flinched and that His plan and words were never altered. He sees and knows all things. He knows the end from the beginning, and hell can't stop Him…no matter how hard they may try!

The Lord recently said to me, *"Don't count Me out. I won't stop until I finish what I started, and even then, I will just begin the next part of My plan so…I will never stop!"*

We're in good hands! Our God knows what He is doing! If we really believe that, then as aware heirs, we will stand our ground and hold fast to our Father's promises! We will not fear!

I once heard Him say:

What you have felt and misunderstood as pressure is actually My grip tightening around you! I have told you and confirmed that My hand is upon you! It's not for show, nor is it to impress people; My hand is upon you because I have claimed you as My own! You are Mine! Now, I have need of that which I have placed in you, so in the days ahead, you will feel My grip getting tighter as I lift you up and draw you closer to Myself so that you can hear My voice and see from My perspective. The tightening of My hand upon you will feel like pressure because My grip will challenge and loose you from emotions and expectations that are not of Me! As you come higher, you will see with clarity and hear with clarity! My voice will become louder than the noise and the chaos around you! My voice will soothe your spirit and calm your soul, and then your eyes will see, and you will know the way, the plan, the intentions of My heart! The lift will be bumpy, the grip will be tight, but I have claimed you. I have led you; now, I will lift you. And you will see how I have arranged the pieces, and you will understand more clearly the process that brought you here. You will see where you've been, understand what I've done, and be renewed with hope and joy and right perspective for what I Am doing and for what I will do!

A good coach will tell you that repetition is one of the greatest tools for learning, for growth, and for increasing strength. It's true for the natural part of us, and it is also true for the spiritual part of us. The more we hear the Lord's instructions and His thoughts concerning us, the more persuaded we will be that we can do what He says. The more we hear His Word, the stronger our faith becomes. The more we call to our remembrance what God has said, the more confidence we will have to obey His leading. So, though repetitious, I feel it is necessary to interject and reiterate some of the things I have already mentioned in previous chapters of this book.

In this moment, Holy Spirit is—and will be—making many of us aware of assignments, opportunities, and strategies that have been reserved and preserved for this time in history. Therefore, we must give the more earnest heed to what He is saying so that, in every moment, we are rightly focused on Him, armed with His Word, and prepared to step in time with His leading.

Some of the assignments He leads us into may be unexpected and could seem very "stretching" for us. With a wrong focus, some may reject the notion that God desires to work through us in these unexpected ways. Others may react to Holy Spirit's leading with a slight hesitation because of a misguided self-evaluation and assessment that seems to suggest that we are incapable of fulfilling these God-ordained tasks. Wrongly surmising that we are unable to do what God is asking us to do and to have what He says that we can have will result in a failure to experience the fullness of all that God has purposed for us to receive and reveal in our times.

Forward advancement requires faith and obedience. It requires us to take our focus off ourselves and refocus on our righteous King. We must grasp the fact that, though we may be incapable within our own strength and ability to be and to do all that He asks us to be and to do, still He is more than enough, and He has granted us access, by His Spirit, to all that He has and is! There is unlimited supply that has been made available to us, and Jesus says that the key to this treasure trove is "faith in God." Faith in God is the game-changer! It takes the pressure of performance off us. When we focus on God, in Whom there is no inability and no lack, we can step into any situation with complete assurance and confident expectation because we know that, by His power, He is well able to do exceeding, abundantly *through* us everything that He has purposed *for* us to do.

God is not asking us to make things happen on our own. He asks us to trust and submit to Him. He will release to us a continuous supply of His Spirit, that will enable us to fulfill every assignment in a way that brings Him glory and recognition. He will be faithful to *complete* in us all that He has *started* in us. There is manifested glory ready to be revealed in ways we have never before known or experienced. God is calling us to focus on Him, trust Him, and go forward!

I hear Him saying:

You can't do it on your own or by your ability! I never asked you to! I said, "Trust Me, and I will reveal ways where you can't see a way!" I said, "I have purpose and assignments for you, and I will go with you as you move forward into the purpose and assignments!" I said, "Don't lean on your understanding. Trust Me, for My thoughts are higher than your thoughts!" I said, "I will liberally give you My wisdom for your advancement!" I said, "I will guide you!" I said, "My Grace is sufficient for you!" I gave you My name (My authority) and My Word! I gave you My Spirit, Who reveals to you My thoughts! I give you My ability which is more than enough to qualify you for where I Am leading you!

You must get this revelation deep inside: I see what you don't see! I know what you don't know! I can do what others—and even you—say cannot be done! I don't just make a way...I AM the Way! I know how to, and will, order your steps to the right places, the right people, the right resources, the right connections...all at the right times! I will open doors that no man can shut! I will promote you and give you increase with no sorrow added to it! I will cause you to BE who and what you've been becoming! Trust Me and fear not. Obey Me beyond your human reasoning. Take the limits off and take those first steps of courageous, uncontaminated faith in Me. As you do, you will witness and experience the unveiling of the path I have chosen that leads you into the fulfillment of My purposes and My hoped-for future. I will reveal My glory to you and manifest My power in you, for you, and through you!

My perfect plan that is exceeding, abundantly, above anything you could ever have thought to imagine is now unfolding! There may be some ravines to cross in the days ahead, but I have already commanded the hosts of Heaven to assist you on your journey. Surrender to Me. Focus on Me. Trust and obey Me...Have faith IN Me! I will get you "there." I will go with you. I will never leave you!

This is our time, and we must show up for this moment. That means that we must be attentive to the Lord. We must be receptive and obedient to His leading. Just as with Joshua, the way ahead may not be easy. As a matter of fact, there may be times when the things He asks us to do look completely impossible, but don't misinterpret difficulties as impossibilities. Remember, with God, all things are possible! Stay focused and completely confident that He Who promised is faithful, and He has you held securely in His grip!

Father, in this transitional moment, we thank You for the memorial stones of all of the past moves of Your Spirit. Thank You for these timeless markers that remind us of Your faithfulness, power, ability and willingness to work through us to carry on with our spiritual inheritance. You are with us! You are for us, and what You did for the previous generations, You will do for us, enabling us to experience Your fullness and pass along the inheritance with even greater weight to impact those who are yet to come!

We trust You, Lord, and we surrender completely to Your grip. Lead us, and we will follow. Speak to us, and we will listen! It is Your will that we desire! Though incapable on our own to accomplish all You may ask us to do, we lean and rely on Holy Spirit to impart to us unlimited supply of strength, wisdom, understanding, favor, and insight. With His help and impartation, we will successfully complete everything You have purposed for us to do.

Our faith is in You, and we will fulfill every assignment in a way that brings all glory and recognition to You. You will complete in us everything that You have started in us! Though the lift may get bumpy, and the way may seem uncertain, we will not fear. Our focus is on You. We step into this unfolding destiny with courage and confident faith in You. We are becoming more and more familiar with Your voice, and another we will not follow! We will see and do all that You have promised for us to see and do in our time. In Jesus' Name! Amen!

10

A Redemptive Movement

[Christ] Who gave Himself for us, that He might redeem us from every lawless deed and purify for Himself His own special people, zealous for good works.

Titus 2:14 NKJV

On January 11, 2022, I had a dream in which I was sitting next to a campfire with Ray Hughes, an anointed minister known for his masterful teaching on the subject of sound. He is also a renowned revival historian. As we sat next to the fire, Ray had a long stick in his hand, and he was using it to stir the embers around the edge of the fire. As he did that, he said, "There's a redemptive sound that is coming that will provoke a redemptive movement in days ahead."

As the dream continued, we conversed about a few other things, and then he said again, "There is a redemptive sound that is coming that will provoke a redemptive movement. It's NOT a LIGHT thing! It's weighty, and it will come forcefully. Hell has tried to stop it, but they won't! *They can't!*"

He then picked up a fairly large rock in his hand, and he stood up. He lifted the rock high above his head and then dropped it right into the middle of the fire. As you can imagine, embers and sparks went flying everywhere. He said very emphatically, "That is what this redemptive movement will be like once the sound is released. It will come hard and fast, and it will cause a response. There will be an instant breaking loose— redemption. The Lord is going to redeem the Church, and He is going to redeem the nation!"

That was the end of the dream.

On Pentecost Sunday 2022, I shared this dream as part of a message I was preaching. The central theme of my message was that God has come to reignite the Church with Pentecostal fire so that our lives and our messages will be presented with demonstration of the Spirit and power, giving the world the ability to see that He is God. Then, just as I was about to conclude the message, there came a sudden, loud, audible *BOOM!* that felt as though it shook the entire building! We later learned that there had been a literal "power surge" that went through the church building. There was no explanation for the surge, and neither the sound equipment nor the electrical system was permanently affected by it. Though it happened suddenly and was *extremely* loud, it didn't even startle most of us! Immediately, several people in the congregation began to weep. It felt as though the presence of the Lord had just sat down on us! We instantly knew that God had just demonstrated to us that He has "dropped the rock" and is now releasing the sound that will provoke an unstoppable redemptive movement!

A Realignment

The dream demonstrated what the movement will look like. Jesus is making a weighty entrance into His Church, and He is dispersing the embers to go in every direction as carriers of the flames of the All-Consuming Fire! Not only is Jesus reclaiming

His Church, but He is reclaiming the nations that His Father gave Him as an inheritance. The nations may rage, and there are those who may plot vain things, but He Who sits in the heavens is releasing the sound of His laughter (Psalm 2), and Jesus, our Rock and our Redeemer, has come to provoke a movement that will change everything!

According to Webster's Dictionary, a meaning of the word *redeem* is "to restore; to renew," which means "to bring back to or put back into a former or original state." I believe we are now in a time when Jesus is redeeming His Church. The Lord once said through a minister, "I made the Church the way I wanted it; now I want the Church the way I made it." Make no mistake about it, the true Church that Jesus "built" is not a weak entity that sits in hiding, hoping to hold on until He returns. He made us to be a glorious Church that is filled and operating with the power of His Spirit. We are called to be filled with His fire and clothed in His glory, marked and known by the demonstration of His awesome might! That was His intention from the very beginning. Now, He's bringing the Church back into alignment with His original purposes, and there will now emerge those carriers of the Fire through whom He will work to initiate the awakening revival that will bring the nation and nations back into alignment with Him. The redemptive movement has started, and hell cannot stop it!

From the prayer rooms of deep and intentional pursuit of the true presence and glory of God, there is emerging a company of true warriors. Filled with wisdom that has been developed by time spent in the Word of God and with fire that has been ignited by His indwelling Spirit, this company is ready and equipped to blaze an undeniable trail of signs, wonders, and miraculous power to capture the attention of the world. As His released firebrands, our goal is not to gain glory and fame for ourselves but to live to exalt Jesus Christ and to make Him known.

It's time for redemption! Jesus is reestablishing us on the foundation of our purpose and existence as His Church, His Body—not to try to redo what has already been done, but to embrace what Jesus started and to receive the mantle that we now are meant to carry for our times. Jesus did not come to the earth to destroy what God had already done; He came to fulfill His earthly part in the plan of God and launch us forth with a deeper revelation and understanding of who God desires for us to be as His heirs.

I challenge you to read the Book of Acts and to put yourself in the storyline. May your spirit be stirred as you read how thousands were saved daily by the preaching of the Word. Multitudes were healed. Governments were influenced with the Gospel. Entire cities and cultures were strongly impacted as the supernatural power of God was revealed through the Church. Many wonders and signs were done. Angels gave assistance to those devoted forerunners. The dead were raised back to life. Evil spirits were cast out of those who were possessed. People were baptized in the Holy Ghost with the evidence of speaking in other tongues. Natural wonders were used by God to assist those who had devoted their lives to His cause. And all of this is just a *very* small portion of the happenings within the movement of the origination of the Church!

These common, ordinary people flowed in uncommon extraordinary power as they carried the glory of God like a blazing fire and left an undeniable mark on history. But was that it? Did Jesus stop working through the Church after the original group was gone? No! The same power, in which they walked to impact the world for their time, is the same power that is extended to us in our time. Their stories are given as a written account of our spiritual heritage. They give us a glimpse of the original model that Jesus came to build.

The transforming power of God that was demonstrated through those Spirit-filled warriors was just the beginning! It is the picture of what the Church was intended to look like. That generation shouts to our generation the revelation of the power that is still available for all who have made Jesus, Lord of their lives!

The Box Top Picture

I like to work jigsaw puzzles. I think it's the challenge of taking all of those pieces that seem, at first, to be nothing more than a pile of colored chunks of cardboard and putting them in their rightful place to form a beautiful picture. Those pieces were formed to fit together. Each piece has a specific place, and when they are connected, they reveal the whole picture of their created intention. One thing I have found in working on these puzzles: it's almost an impossible task to put them together without the box top that reveals the picture of what it's intended to look like once it's completed. If you don't have the picture, the pieces make no sense. The picture gives you the pattern for what you are piecing together.

Along with the life of Jesus, the Book of Acts provides a "box-top picture" for the Church. It is the reality and revelation of what we are supposed to look and be like—a functioning body *"joined and knit together by what every joint supplies, according to the effective working by which every part does its share"* to reveal the *"the likeness of Christ"* (see Ephesians 4:13, 16). Anything less than what is revealed in the Book of Acts is not a complete picture of the Church that Jesus built us to be. Acts was the beginning. Now, we are the continuation of what was begun. We are the pieces, and as we each do our part, the picture of the reality of

Jesus is revealed through us, giving the world indisputable and unavoidable evidence of His existence, power, and love.

This has been true throughout history. Every generation has a part in God's plan, and when each does its part, the "mantle" grows and gets passed along as a viable, valuable heritage. This allows subsequent generations to know what belongs to them so that they too can take their place in the picture that reveals Christ.

Where we have been content to congregate in our buildings and burn, at best, as a small flame, the Rock, Christ Jesus, is "dropping" into His Church and stirring the embers. He is releasing the sound of the rushing wind that is pushing us forth to burn and shine for His glory. In doing so, He is provoking this "redemptive movement" in our time. He is bringing us back into alignment so that we can reveal the true picture of the Church, functioning as living examples of the model that He has always intended us to be. He is stirring up individual purposes on the inside of us like fire shut up in our bones. He is blowing on the fire to intensify its fervency, causing us to pursue Him with undaunted willingness to obey His leading...no matter the cost. We will not settle in complacency. We feel the urgency of this moment. We see the picture, we know our "piece" fits to help form the whole, and we are provoked by Holy Spirit to get "in place" and be!

Dip Your Pen in the Ink

Whether we realize it or not, each one of us is passing along an inheritance of some sort. We must be diligent to hear and obey God so that the inheritance we carry and will leave is the one that God intended for us to pass along.

Each generation should be showing to the generations to come the praises of the Lord, His strength, and His wonderful works that He has done so that they might know them and that they may arise and declare them to their children. Knowledge of God and demonstration of His goodness and power will cause them to set their hope in God and not forget His works (see Psalms 78:2-7).

There is a Scripture in Psalms that I have always loved, and to me, it is very thought-provoking. A portion of Psalm 90:9 KJV says, "*We spend our years as a tale that is told.*" That means that the years of our lives are paragraphs and chapters of a story that is being written by our actions or by our refusal to act, by our faith in God or by our rejection of Him, by our fear or by our trust in God. Our decisions, our conversations, our actions, our responses to life's situations, our living, our relationship with the Lord or lack thereof—all of this is writing a story for the next generation to read. Some are "reading" *as* we "write," and some will still read our stories long after we are gone. The great and sobering question is, what are we writing? What story are we leaving for the following generations? Will our lives "write" the story of a life lived for Christ? Will the story be convincing enough that those who read it may receive the baton and run on with it?

Our sincere prayer and decree before God should be: "Take my life and let it be consecrated, Lord, to Thee! I surrender myself to You! My heart is the pen of a ready writer." We must set ourselves to listen to all that the Lord is revealing. We must not allow ourselves to be so captivated by what the devil is doing that we become distracted and step away from our posts and our part in the plan of God. We must keep our hearts turned toward Him so that we can hear what He is saying, and then we must cooperate with Holy Spirit as He enables us to do what God shows to us to do.

147

I remember as a freshman in high school that one of the extra-curricular courses that we were offered was a class in which we learned the art of calligraphy. Each student was given one of the unique pens, along with their various sizes of tips and a bottle of ink. I was so enthralled by this new-found writing technique. It was very different from the normal flow of a regular ink pen. The pen had to be held correctly. The movement of the hand and the position of the tip is what determined the outcome of the writing. If done correctly, the result would be a beautifully written script that was captivating, demanding the attention of the one who would read it. However, the outcome would have been very different without the bottle of ink! Without the ink, there would be no script!

God has given us His Word and countless examples of the moving of His Spirit throughout history to provide us with understanding and revelation of His willingness and desire to work through our lives to demonstrate His power and glory. I am so thankful for the Word of God and for the written records that give us this glorious knowledge of what He has done throughout the generations! But it wasn't recorded just so we can "ooh and ahh" over the things we read, as though that's all there is! No! "*Whatsoever things were written aforetime were written for our learning*" (Romans 15:4 KJV). God gives us, through these recorded accounts, the understanding of Who He is and how He moves. That understanding enlightens us with the revelation that there are no limitations to His power! Now, we are the pen in His skillful hand, and He has given us the "ink" of His recorded history to fill us with the ability to be used to continue to write His story!

I once heard the Lord say:

You will dip your pen in the ink of past movements.
You will feel what they felt and learn what they

148

experienced with greater detail than you have known before. Then through you, I will continue to write the story. The rest of the story will be told, seen, and experienced, and if you think the beginning was good…just wait until you see the rest!

This is a word for the Church. The time for redemption, the restoration of the original model, has come. The original is what God has intended all along. We don't have to try to recreate what happened in the beginning. That part of the story has already been written. It's redemption, not duplication. We must become a manifestation of the original by surrendering fully to Holy Spirit as He continues to reveal the fullness of Christ to us and through us.

God says to the Church, *"Return to Me…and I will return to you"* (Zechariah 1:3). As we, the Church, the Bride of Christ, stir ourselves and return to Him with our whole hearts, our eyes will behold Him. In the beauty and splendor of His glory, we will encounter Him, hear Him, and be drawn to Him, alone. And not only will those encounters impact us, but His Light will shine through us, and those in darkness will see Him. Then, it will be in America and in the world as it was on Mount Carmel when Elijah stood and released fervent, faith-filled prayer and decrees that provoked the demonstration of the power and glory of God. From 1 Kings 18:39 KJV we read:

> *When all the people saw [the demonstrated glory and power of God], they fell on their faces; and they said, 'The Lord, He is God; the Lord, He is God'*

That's an awakening…and that is what will CHANGE EVERYTHING!

When people see the demonstrated glory and power of God, they will know that He is real, and it will awaken a hunger inside them to know Him for themselves. This is how the world will be changed. This is how nations will be saved. We must first have a spiritual reviving in the Church, and as we step into the full manifestation of the sons and daughters of God, a spiritual awakening to an awareness of God will come to the nations.

God is redeeming the Church. He is restoring and bringing us back into alignment with His original purpose: that we shine as unmistakable ambassadors of Christ, who are fully demonstrating His likeness to the world. Our focus is fixed on Christ, and our desire is that He will reach through us to change hearts! We are called to be those vessels so filled with Christ's anointing that everywhere we go, He reaches through our very lives to smear the atmosphere with His unavoidable presence. This will allow those in darkness to experience His love and power, awakening them to an awareness of Him. As the hearts of mankind are turned back to God, transformation will then come to our culture, cities, homes, schools, governments, regions, territories, and nations.

The Lord is calling the Church to turn back to Him, to become aware of and receive our valuable inheritance, and to be ignited with the fire of God to shine the Light of Christ to a very dark world. Those who have gone before us received the mantle of this spiritual inheritance, and they carried it for their time, demonstrating the reality of Jesus, and impacting the world with the evidence of His undeniable power and glory! Now, it's our time. The Word of God, His will and testament, reveals the splendor of our rich inheritance. We must receive it, and carry on with it.

For all who will say "yes" to His invitation to receive our inherited portion, Holy Spirit will activate the fullness of that which we have been entrusted to carry. To all who will yield their lives to Him as a pen in His hand, He will release the oil, and through us, He will continue to write the story—His story—so that those around us and the generations yet to come may be made aware of what is being extended to them. May the demonstration of His power that is revealed through our obedience and submission to Him be so real and evident that it sparks a passion in subsequent generations and provokes them to take their place on the timeline and carry on with God's original intentions.

Father, it's not by our might or strength that we can receive and carry on with this amazing inheritance with which we have been entrusted. We cannot do it on our own, but by Your Spirit, we can become vessels through which You can reveal Your glory. We are enthralled by You! We pursue You! We will remain focused on You! We are wholly devoted to You and to Your righteous cause. By the empowerment of Your Holy Spirit, we will carry and release the anointing that will draw men to the saving knowledge of Christ. We humble ourselves before You, and we each sincerely say, "All of me for all of You! Finish what You have started."

Teach us, Lord, to wisely invest this spiritual inheritance so that we may pass it along to the generations who will follow us. May they see in us a true example that will ignite the ember that is within them, that they, too, may run with the fire and see the continuation of Your original intentions.

Though it may seem to some that the nation and the Church are too far gone and that there is no hope of redemption, we know that You still reign. Your eternal plan of the ages has not diminished, and You have not altered the purposes that You breathed and prophesied into the Church and the nation. Now, You are calling both back into alignment with You. Though darkness has covered the earth and gross darkness has shrouded many people, we are completely persuaded that You have released the redemptive sound that is now stirring and awakening the Body of Christ. Out of the ashes we are rising to shine with the unavoidable light of Your transforming glory. You have clothed us with Your righteousness. You have filled us with Your Spirit, and now we are emerging with the wisdom to utilize the weapons of our warfare. These weapons are not carnal, but mighty through You, our God, to pull down every stronghold and to break the powers of hell and their attempts to stop this redemptive movement.

We yield our lives to You, and we declare that the seeds which You have sown into us will spring forth and bear the fruit of Your purposes! We will surrender to You and allow the story to continue to be written through our lives. We rise above the noise of the chaos surrounding us—and even above the influence of our own emotions—and we set our focus on You. We listen for Your instructions, and we will obey You swiftly. We will work with Holy Spirit as He guides us according to Your great wisdom. We will stand under the weight of Your glory, and those who sit in darkness will see and be drawn to Your great light and be changed by the redeeming power of salvation through Your Son, Jesus! In the name and authority of Jesus, we pray! Amen.

About the Author

GINA ENTERED A PERSONAL RELATIONSHIP with the Lord Jesus Christ at a young age. Fully surrendering her life to the Lord, she was launched into a journey toward fulfilling her God-given purposes.

Gina has served in ministry for over forty years. She is a prophetic minister, a revivalist at heart, who ministers under the anointing and power of the Holy Spirit. Through preaching, prayer, and prophetic declaration, she is contending for an awakening to an awareness of God that will lead to revival and reformation in the Church and in the nation. Gina walks in integrity, seeking only to please the Lord. Her desire is to always honor and bring glory to Jesus Christ alone.

Gina is also a prophetic dreamer. Her dreams and visions have been, and are being, used as strategy for prayer, prayer assignments, and insight to assist the Church in taking Her place to bring an awakening to God in America. Dutch Sheets, Tim Sheets, Chuck Pierce, and others have given voice to many of her dreams and visions in their conferences and ministry platforms by sharing them in their messages, books, social media posts, and podcasts.

Gina is the author of *Awakening the Church to Awaken a Nation*, and *Dreams of Awakening*. She is a native and lifetime resident of the great state of Tennessee.

More by Gina Gholston

Awakening the Church to Awaken a Nation

In *Awakening the Church to Awaken a Nation*, Gina Gholston shares prophetic dreams, visions, and prophetic insights that have been given to her by God for the purpose of revealing wisdom and strategy concerning His intentions for our times and for our nation. The words of this book will challenge you to know your identity in Christ and to listen above the chaos to hear God's Kingdom strategies that are being poured out by Holy Spirit in our times.

Dreams of Awakening

In *Dreams of Awakening*, Gina Gholston presents detailed dreams and visions she has received from the Lord, along with their interpretations. Each of the prophetic revelations highlights a resounding call for the Body of Christ to rise and shine as lights in darkness. Each chapter features a powerful prophetic dream and corresponding prayer activation, helping you wage warfare prayer to bring about His promises of awakening.

To order, please visit Gina's website:
www.ginagholstonministries.org

You can also order Gina's books via Amazon.com.

Contact Info

Mailing Address

Gina Gholston
P.O. Box 30781
Clarksville, TN 37040

Email

ggministries20@gmail.com

Website

www.ginagholstonministries.org

Facebook

www.facebook.com/ginagholstonministries/

Truth Social

ginagholston@ginagholston

YouTube Channel

Gina Gholston Ministries

Made in the USA
Las Vegas, NV
25 June 2023

73892109R00095